The Kahuna and I

Bill and I welcome you to share in our story

The Kahuna and I

A REMARKABLE TRUE HAWAIIAN STORY BY
VICTORIA KAPUNI

The Kahuna and I: A remarkable True Hawaiian Story
by Victoria Kapuni

ISBN 978-1-64271-067-0 (Paperback)
ISBN 978-1-64271-087-8 (Hard Cover)
ISBN 978-1-64271-076-2 (Digital)

Printed in the United States of America.

Okir Publishing, Inc.
1718 Capitol Avenue
Cheyenne, WY 82001
https://okir-publishing.com

ACKNOWLEDGEMENTS

I thank my editor, Deborah Herman, for her organizing, deleting and other skills that she brought to the editing process of this book. We were blessed for our spiritual connection.

Thank you, my brother, William P. Gillespie IV for always being there for me. We are truly blessed to be brother and sister.

Thank all of you with whom I have connected in both great and small duration and magnitude throughout my life. You have helped me on my path, and I am, indeed, exceedingly grateful. Bless you all.

I am profoundly blessed to have found and been the wife of William Ku a Mo'o Helelani Kealoha Kapuni to whom I dedicate this book.

CONTENTS

LIST OF GRAPHICS

INTRODUCTION

I WROTE THIS BOOK SO THAT others who find that they don't "fit in" where they are in time and space or situation of birth; and hence, feel like they don't belong anywhere and are alone in that place, can have solace in knowing that if they follow their path, everything will turn out all right. Life is a mystery and we need to forge our way through our journey, through births, deaths, jobs, marriages, relationships with people along the way. We need to just ride it through, and experience all the joys, as well as the great sadness that comes our way...all the while looking for the light that leads us to the ultimate end of this physical human life.

Some of us will be luckier than others in what we choose to experience. Some will lead no risk lives and choose what I call predicable ones. Others will seek out varied experiences within their own spiritual, ethical and moral parameters given the fact that the experiences may lead to adventure....all dependent on our intensions. Each experience, no matter how painful or wonderful, is an experience we are blessed with in our learning. For life in this earthly existence is one of learning and evolving into becoming the great spiritual beings that we are! We simply have to recognize and develop within each of us our extraordinary capabilities. We need to actualize the spiritual potential within each of us while we are here on earth.

The key I believe is to proceed through our lives without fear. We have so many fears to face during these material lives on earth... the fear of death being the biggest one. This is the ultimate fear isn't it? The fear of death and the demise of our material bodies we have spent a life time living in and learning about? For those who travel a more spiritual path and face death of the body with the strength of a warrior, acceptance, courage, dignity, peace do so because they spent a good bit of their lives here living in spirit. The spiritual world is the living world…the world we are born from and the world to which we go when we leave. The physical world is the one that is matter which constantly changes its form as atoms move into different physical and chemical configurations forming different environments.

Once you realize you are 'different' from others, simply accept it and continue on your path towards the destiny you choose to follow. Don't try and be like everyone else. Don't try and fit in. Don't try to change the wondrous human being you are because you think you will feel better if you look more and act more like everyone else.

Learn courage to accept your 'differentness' and continue your path and discover the wonderful gifts you have been blessed with. The gifts are what make you so unique and different and by accepting them, you are enabling yourself to live your path and continue your marvelous adventure and find everything you are seeking in every way. Like I did.

PART I

CHAPTER ONE

HOW DOES A PHILADELPHIA DEBUTANTE, SCHOOLED, groomed and taught all the refined and courteous manners of high society end up in Kaunakakai, Molokai, married to an almost full-blooded Hawaiian, the love of her life? In the autumn of my journey, after years of broken relationships, and heartache, I found my twin soul in a man who knew my spirit even if he could hardly speak my language. My life had been debutante balls, three marriages and a law practice. His had been 'raising up' in a grass shack on the beaches of Oahu, diving off cliffs, catching fish and game from the ocean and aina (land) and guarding the sacred ways of his people.

Although Ke Akua (God) gave us a relatively short time on this plane, I know that we looked for each other our whole lives. We always knew we were blessed to find each other, and never took the treasure we had found for granted. We taught each other some of the most important mysteries of this beautiful planet and Island I now call my home. Through our love I now continue my journey and pass the torch of his Mana to you. This is our story.

As a young girl I never went anywhere without heels and hose, a hat, white gloves and maybe a string of pearls. My clothes were tailored from the Sports and Specialty or Nana's shop. I was from "old moneyed" Chestnut Hill, Pennsylvania and there were rules that were simply not to be broken.

Breeding they called it. We girls were taught all those special ways of doing things like setting a place at a table with three or four drinking glasses, two or three spoons, two or three knives and three or four forks depending on what was to be served; or how to wipe our napkins at either corner of our mouths or stand and courtesy when

3

an elder walked into the room. We learned the subjects you 'did not speak about in public' as well as the subjects suitable for dinner conversation. We took ballet lessons, music lessons, and ball room dancing lessons learning not only the steps but how to maneuver big skirts with hoop undergarments underneath, so our skirts wouldn't fly up over our heads when we sat down. Then, of course, for school and everywhere else we wore full skirts with from 5 to 8 crinolines worn underneath depending on the fullness of the skirt.

We were taught to appreciate finely carved mahogany furniture, Waterford crystal, English bone china, Irish linens, oriental rugs from Turkey or China, English Tudor grey, granite stone mansions with ten bedrooms in them like the one I grew up in. We were groomed to appreciate all the finer 'things' money can buy and the gentlemen husbands to go along with the money....the ones who played golf or tennis on grass courts at the country clubs. Everyone belonged to a country club and it 'mattered' which one that was. The old money country club was the Philadelphia Cricket Club (the one my family belonged to), which was the best, because the old moneyed families believed it to be.

An old moneyed family husband was a much better trophy than that of a new money family. The new money people, someone like Bill Gates, would not have the breeding and pedigree to go along with the money. This was never so apparent as during Debutante season.

Debutante season began during your senior year of High School. The actual parties were scheduled for June, but the acceptance process to the June Ball began during the preceding fall and was completed by January.

Dancing with my Father at the June Ball

To be accepted by the Philadelphia Social Society Committee your parents had to submit "pedigree" information to show how far back your ancestors went as far as living in America. I was a Daughter of the American Revolution (DAR) meaning that my ancestors were traced back to living in America before the American Revolution. My maternal Grandfather's ancestors came over on the second wave of ships from England to Plymouth Rock; and my paternal Grandmother's ancestors traced back to before the early 1700s from

England. She is one of the two DAR connections I have in my early eastern United States societal background.

My dad was born in Altoona Pennsylvania; but his father, a medical doctor, moved to Philadelphia when he was quite young. I never knew my paternal grandfather, who was apparently a benevolent care giving physician (7th generation of first son physicians), who went to patient's homes when they were sick. During the flu epidemic of the 1920s he worked tirelessly caring for the sick but eventually died of the disease. My father grew up without a dad and his mother was so bitter over her husband's death, she did not allow either of her two sons to go to medical school and take a chance they would also die while tending to the sick like their father had done.

Both my paternal grandparents came from a long lineage of early settlers to America. My paternal grandfather's family migrated to America from Aberdeen, Scotland at least ten generations ago. His ancestors had acquired Scottish family lands from the King in the 1100's. On a visit to Scotland, I discovered the family name is everywhere in Edinburgh -- streets, schools, shops etc.

My maternal grandfather, whom I knew, had relatives fighting and dying on both sides of the Civil War (one dying in Andersonville prison camp). He was a learned man who taught Greek and Latin in a university before becoming a Methodist minister and eventually changing his religion to Christian Science with my grandmother.

My grandmother was a school teacher living in Minnesota when she met my grandfather. She was four years older than my grandfather, which my mother only discovered after she died. It would have been very unusual at the turn of the century for a wife to be older then her husband.

Her lineage was three quarter English and one quarter German. She was a relative newcomer, as far as my ancestors were concerned, coming to America; but she liked to tell a story of her girlhood when a band of Indians in war paint came to her family's Minnesota homestead while her father was away, and her mother went out to them carrying food. After she gave them the food, they left.

My grandmother influenced my non-violent peaceful attitude towards animals particularly, but people and the world as well. My lesson occurred one Christmas after I had purchased (with my own saved up money and gave to her) a silk scarf with fringe on it. I thought it was beautiful because it was embroidered with mallards on a lake with lake plants all around. The problem was there was a man with a rifle in his hand in the embroidery-- apparently a hunter. She then took stitch by stitch out, the rifle, removing it from the picture.

She was also my introduction to the sanctity of nature and the expansive beauty of the earth and sky and respect for all living things. My grandparents took me out to fields of wild flowers and grassy hills and woods with them. They introduced me to nature when I was very young. I remember as a little girl, four or five, sitting in a field of grass holding yellow buttercups in my hands shaped as a bowl for the flowers to lay in. They opened my eyes to the natural beauty of the world and how it is a living life force all around us.

They gave me a sense of nature, but they also gave me my pedigree. And once you passed the pedigree test, the money test was next.

It was then and probably is now very expensive to become a debutante. The cost of the June Ball, the largest debutante party in Philadelphia at the time could be the equivalent of one half a year at college for a few hours out of one evening in June. I didn't realize it at the time, but this was one of the happiest times I ever had with my mother. My mother had the pedigree, but her family did not have the money. My mother had the proper, reserved, provincial and puritanical ways of a pedigreed WASP woman, but even she couldn't help getting swept up in the excitement.

Once accepted, each of us had a set period of time to make out our guest lists to be submitted to the committee for approval. We each could invite 100 guests who could bring their escorts. There were approximately sixteen senior young ladies from Philadelphia chosen for this event, which signified the announcement by their parents that they were eligible for dating and marriage. The phrase was their "coming out," party. We were now to officially take our places among the members of society.

We were also sending out a message to the society boys that we were the ladies society would deem worthy for them and their standing in the community. What I didn't realize at the time was, it was a way to keep the wealth among the wealthy.

I went to a prestigious private girls' school at the time called Springside. There were three of us chosen to be debutantes from Springside that year so we divided up the class to make sure everyone was invited to the ball between us. I remember there was a discussion about the two Jewish girls in our class, but at the time I didn't understand why. I never saw them as any different from me. We were all friends at school so I didn't understand the muffled whispers about whether or not they should be excluded from the Ball. I made sure they were invited on my list and my parents didn't seem to question it.

Looking back, I think my parents had a bigger problem with Catholics then Jews. I remember heated comments about the new catholic President. I played golf at the Cricket Club, and there were not many young women playing at the time. I was also athletically talented and could keep up almost stroke for stroke with most of the boys so I played with them. I was junior girls' champion of the Philadelphia Cricket Club two years in a row. But the real advantage of my playing with the boys was I played better golf trying to keep up with them. Some were Catholic boys from Villanova. One asked me out and when I asked my parents if I could go and told them he was Catholic, I was told flatly, "You cannot go out with him." I tried to object but no discussion was allowed.

It seemed like such an arbitrary decision that I complained to my friends about it. One friend thought of a plan that I would go to her house for the night and the boy could pick me up from and bring me back to her house for a date. I went out with him but because I felt uneasy throughout the date, having disobeyed my parents' wishes, I never saw him again. I didn't know why I wasn't supposed to go out with him, but I certainly didn't like disobeying my parents, and I never tried it again.

That senior year was a whirlwind of activity. My mother and I got along and she seemed happy as she shopped for and chose the many beautiful dresses I wore for the special parties. Before she had married my dad, she had been a model and dress buyer for a Philadelphia

Department store. Every few days I would come home from school and find a new dress my mother had bought for me lying on my bed. She enjoyed surprising me, and I enjoyed her attention. I never felt good enough in her presence. She had typically been critical of many things about me and about many things in life period. She was now completely in her element – parties and dresses. I loved seeing myself wearing the new dresses in the mirror. We had a happy time together.

My Mother

There were so many different types of parties to go to that year. There were brunches, lunches, teas, dinners and dances all leading up to the June Ball. One of the dresses my mother bought me she referred to as "French." All I know is that it made me feel uneasy, because it had small white lace ruffles sewed across the scooped neck in a way to enhance the curve of your bust. I had never worn anything like that, but noticed a lot more attention from boys. Even though I liked that it had a blue taffeta mid-calf length skirt that swirled, I wasn't quite ready for the gawking attention from the boys.

My favorite evening dress was a strapless pink chiffon trimmed with pink embroidered roses around the bust. For brunch or an informal dance I had the most beautiful dress that was like poetry in motion. It held my small 21" waist in with a cumber bund, reached just below the knees and had a ruffle that now reminds me of a fat Hawaiian lei. It provided just enough weight that the skirt swayed beautifully whenever I walked and moved. It was such a difference from the tom boy way I would usually dress and feel. I was shy and often felt invisible in a room. But with these dresses I felt pretty.

These parties were a test of our breeding and we were observed throughout them all. The Teas especially had expectations that we would dress and comport ourselves as proper ladies. Dresses for teas covered your shoulders with sleeves and had conservative necklines over which you wore pearls or some other conservative classic necklace. If a jacket was worn over the dress, a pin was worn on the lapel. The afternoon dresses could have jackets to cover a sleeveless dress or they could be suits. All ensembles demanded stockings and appropriate footwear. This meant no spiked heels. Two inch heeled shoes with matching bags were fine. If the parties were after Memorial Day white heels were appropriate. After Labor Day white heels were completely inappropriate. Handbags were beaded for eveningwear and white leather, linen or other appropriate material for day parties...no straw or shoulder bags.

My schedule that June was hectic. There were times when there were four parties scheduled in one day. There might be a brunch, tea, dinner and then a dance. The day of the June Ball was extraordinary. My mother and I went to the hairdresser together to get our hair washed and set in the style of the times. My father took my ball gown and accoutrement to the Bellevue Stratford Hotel in downtown Philadelphia where the ball was to be held at ten that evening. I primped and dressed with one of my girlfriends, who would be staying with me at the hotel for the night after the ball. Then I went to the preparatory room for the debs where we lined up to get our flower fans that we would be holding and dancing with and to get our instructions for how we would make our grand entrance. There were sixteen of us being presented to society that evening and each one of us were going to have to singularly descend a very steep marble set of stairs with a spotlight upon us as they announced how proud our parents were to introduce us to them. I know each of us were focused on keeping our footing because the two storied marble stairs (starting at the balcony of the ballroom) were curved and were smaller at one end than the other.

At the bottom of the stairs as the twenty-five piece band played, our fathers would approach us and dance with us. My Dad and I had practiced dancing together a lot and it was a very loving and proud moment for us. The protocol was then that your primary escort would cut in and dance with you and then your secondary escort would cut in. Then the next Deb would do the same thing and we wouldn't exhale until she was safely on the ground.

After the Debs were safe everyone could dance together and everyone could have fun, including family members such as Aunts, Uncles and Cousins who had all come out to share the occasion. As I look back, I remember my grandmother, who sat in the balcony with my family for my coming out party, listened to all of my excitement about all the parties and the festivities. I wanted to share with her all of it. Her only comment was, "the higher you ride, the greater the fall".

—ɯ—

My younger days at private school were not all parties and joy. I couldn't read! I had a high IQ so I was able to learn most of what I needed. People didn't know much about dyslexia in those days. I know my mother (when I was a baby) made me change from being left handed to being right handed so I would "fit in" better. I always wondered if it crossed my circuits to interfere with nature that way, but I would likely have been dyslexic without her interference.

I didn't learn how to read until 8th grade. My fifth grade teacher figured out something was wrong with my reading capabilities; but she thought I was retarded. When the IQ tests proved otherwise my parents looked for people who could help me read.

They finally found a psychologist, at Chestnut Hill Academy, my brother's boy's school, who had just discovered the existence of dyslexia and was running summer reading camps for children to teach them how to read. I acquired some self esteem knowing what was 'wrong' with me and seeing that there were others struggling with the same thing.

That summer was also significant in my mind, because for some reason I drew three pictures on pieces of paper that I hung with scotch tape on my wallpapered walls in my bedroom, much to my mother's dismay. They were pencil drawings and each portrayed a large, good looking man protecting a woman with his arms outstretched holding a blanket around her. It sort of looked like they had both been through a disaster of some sort...a hurricane maybe.

I kept those pencil drawings for years and years. I loved looking at those pictures at the time and pretended a man would be there for me sometime in my life to protect me. After my Hawaiian husband and I started 'going together' and planned our wedding, I remarked to him about those pictures and described them to him. It was strange that they would be so prominent in my mind after so many decades of not being in my mind at all. My husband was very much a Hawaiian warrior and protector; and we had both been through severe storms in our lives.

CHAPTER TWO

I ALWAYS FELT DIFFERENT FROM MY peers. It wasn't just that I couldn't read even though I was very smart. In my co-ed grade school, the girls had to play dumb so the boys would like them. That wasn't easy for me to do. I didn't like it because I was being dishonest with the boy by manipulating him the same way I had seen my mother 'work' men around her finger. I felt it was disrespectful to the boy to 'play him for a fool', so I chose not to play that game. I became very direct and to the point in all conversations with people from then on.

Oil Painting of me when I was in 4th grade

One day in fourth grade while attending Germantown Friends School, the secretary to the principal of the upper school (high school) came into the class and asked me to go outside with her.

I followed her and she asked me if I was a Christian Scientist, and I said, "yes".

She asked me if I knew how to heal, and I said, "yes". She said that a lady in the lunchroom had just had a heart attack, and she was a Christian Scientist and refused all medical care and asked for a Christian Scientist practitioner. The Secretary to the Principle asked me if I could help her. I said, "yes".

I was only ten-years-old, but I was confident I would be able to heal her. I received my first bible (King James version) and Science and Health with Key to the Scriptures from my grandparents on my birthday at the age of 7. My grandparents were both Christian Science Healers and leaders in the Second Church of Christ Scientist in Philadelphia. This was a huge church constructed with large blocks of polished granite in the inside (similar in size to those used for the Egyptian Pyramids) and red brick on the outside.

There was a giant organ which my grandmother played when she was not a 'reader'. A reader is like a minister, only the words are totally taken from the Bible and Science and Health book. No ad lib or commentary is done. It is all Bible and Science and Health reading. I had been going to Sunday school, and had learned from my grandparents, who were the leaders of this huge church with many hundreds of people as members.

On Sundays, we had church and then dinners at either my grandmother's home or at our house. We all traveled together in my grandfather's blue Desoto sedan to and from church; and stopped at a neighborhood drug store where my grandfather would buy a Sunday paper and lifesavers for my brother and me.

My Grandmother was the most influential person for me at this time. My mother was lacking in nurturing qualities and from this perspective and time and space, I can see that her erratic behavior and temper made me lacking in a good sense of self. My mother was a very pretty woman--a fashion model as a matter of fact...blond hair and green eyes and an unbelievable body. I don't know if she knew how to leave the center of attention to focus on her child. My grandmother was my saving grace in nurturing and loving me… the person I was inside.

My Grandmother

I had literally learned at her knee how she prayed and healed people over the phone which was what she often did when I visited her. She made her living healing people. When I was little, we only lived a few blocks from her house so I was over there most of the time to get away from my mother. She would always serve tea at 4:00 pm and something freshly baked from the oven like cookies, cake or scones. She always had canned jams too because growing up on a farm, all food was canned for the winter and she carried on that way of life even though she was living in a city now.

I walked into the room following the secretary. It was in the basement of the school. The walls were painted an ugly green which was better than the grey cement floor and the ill woman, small, was laying on a bed. There was one tiny little window in the room, and it was high on the wall where the bed was. The secretary got me a chair to sit on, and I sat down next to the bed facing her and began praying. I remember the sunlight shown down on us through the window as a shaft of light poured in on me. I have no idea how long I prayed, but at some point, the woman sat up, thanked me, stood up and walked out the door to go to the kitchen and finish cooking for the kids' lunch. She was a lunchroom worker and returned to her duties as if nothing had happened at all. I wasn't surprised.

The secretary, however, was amazed and took me upstairs to the 'big part' of the school where the big kids were and walked me behind the short wooden banister, which separated the secretaries, headmaster and assistant headmaster from the general populous of the high school. She told me to sit in a chair and wait. She went behind the big white wooden door with the bright brass door knob. She came out and asked me to come in which I did. Low and behold…it was Mr. Scattergood, the Headmaster of the whole school, and I was only ten years old!

They asked me to sit down…this time it was in a big wooden chair with upholstered cushions and my feet didn't touch the floor. The floor was dark wood made with very wide wood planks eight to ten inches wide.

The Headmaster asked me, "How did you heal that woman?" I responded, "I prayed".

He asked again and I said, "I prayed".

Then he asked me "what do you mean you prayed?"

I replied innocently, "God is perfect and he is our father and we are his children. We are all made in the image and likeness of God and therefore we are perfect beings like God. God has no disease, there can be no disease in us either because we are his children. The illness you appear to have is an illusion and not real."

He kept asking me more questions and I couldn't answer them any differently than "I prayed". I just kept saying all I did was pray and that didn't seem to be a good enough answer for him.

I was a healer from Christian Science teachings. Being any kind of healer other than a medical doctor, was uncommon in those days. This was an event in my life that made it clear to me, in just one more instance, how different I really was.

CHAPTER THREE

My Father

MY DAD WAS PROUD OF MY athletic accomplishments and came to a lot of my hockey, basketball and Lacrosse games. We would often play in father and daughter-golf tournaments also; and when I played in a tournament by myself, he would practice with me at night before the next day's match. He was very supportive of me at all times, he just wasn't around as much as I wanted him to be. He traveled what seemed like half the time or more some years…

depending on the work I guess, or maybe my Mother's mood. He was an executive vice president of hardware companies. One company made saws and chainsaws another hammers and other tools.

My father loved fish. My father loved to catch them in the ocean and lakes, and he loved to raise tropical fish. He had a room on the 3rd floor of the house where he raised hundreds and hundreds of fish in 100 gallon aquariums. One day under the weight of the heavy aquariums, the two by four stands he had built broke and the aquariums came crashing down on one another breaking the glass and releasing the 100s of gallons of water onto the floor which then cascaded down the staircase, carrying the fish flopping on the steps and on the floor, as the water flowed. That was the tail end of the fish hobby.

Another hobby he had was flowers. He grew them outside in flower beds and inside the house where he set them on trays which he placed in the large windowsills. Our windowsills were very deep about one and a half to two feet deep because of how the old pre-Revolutionary houses were built with very thick walls in the basement (in our house about six feet wide) and then taper to thinner thickness as you go up the house until at the top, (third floor in our house) it was of a normal size wall and windowsill thickness about four inches.

He often spoke about going to Hawaii because many of his friends were traveling there and speaking of its flowers and breathtaking ocean beauty. Because he told me of these things, I always had in the back of my mind to go to Hawaii. My father was my first and best friend.

Because my Dad was a business man, I took subjects in college that would enable me to have conversations with him and understand what he did at his job. That's the whole reason I majored in Economics at Ohio State…so I could intelligently talk with my father about matters that were important to him. The whole reason I chose Law School over medical school was because I remember my Dad once telling me that if he had it to do over again, he would have chosen law school instead of University of Pennsylvania Wharton School of Business. I asked him why and he said attorneys for the company made more money for less work than he did.

My Dad taught me about hard work by example. He left the house at 6:45 am and returned at 6:30pm. While he attended Wharton Night School and graduated as valedictorian, he worked a full- time day job!

My best friends were boys. I suppose because my father and I were such good friends. When I was in high school, a group of boys, a year older then me used to hang out at my house sometimes on the weekends. We'd talk and then they would take off somewhere. They would come over if they had a problem or sometimes to just say "hello". One time, one of our friends fell off the bumper of his MG and hit his head on a rock and died. I remember the sadness still yet. I learned how fragile life is and it can be gone in a moment. I tried to live in the now for the present and did for a while until tragedies began to hit me fast and furiously.

My Grandfather

In my junior year of High School, I was finally asked out by a very nice young man whom I had admired from afar for a long time. While I was getting ready the night of our first date to a big dance at his boy's school, my grandfather passed away. My grandfather was the strong silent type man; whom I did not know very well because he rarely spoke. He sat in a chair in the living room and listened to the family gathered around him and was very English, showing emotion only on rare occasions. I always kissed his bald head because I was told it made him happy. It did. He'd smile at me afterwards.

I never knew how smart he was, because he rarely spoke…a man of few words my brother would always say. He was a humble man and went about his business in quietness. The only thing I remember him getting upset about was when he found out his long time golfing partner cheated on his golf score. That sorely disappointed him. But he was quiet about it. He was a spiritual man.

My Pop Pop's passing was a quiet one for me. I worked through it with my spiritual beliefs and then got caught up in my living. It was the death of my grandmother my freshman year of college that knocked me down and damaged my faith. I was beginning to doubt how there was a loving God who would take her away from me, and I struggled with this loss. I remember a lot of anger at God for taking her. We had moved to Columbus, Ohio and I hadn't seen her or called her, because I was away at college. She had held me when I was little and made me feel safe….so safe with her like nothing could ever hurt me.

I went to college in Arizona my freshman year, but it was difficult for me because I was 'different' and did not 'fit in'. It was known as a party school and I didn't drink, smoke or take drugs like some of them did. I was often called names like "Pollyanna" and "prude' and 'goodie two shoes" and "snob". In addition, I couldn't read and was a Christian Scientist.

I continued to be unable to read (only 6-10 pages an hour depending on the subject material); yet, I had to pretend I was a normal reader. If I went to every single class, understood what went on in class, and took notes, I did well in school. No one could tell

I wasn't reading the material. I had an auditory memory as well as a visual memory, so I didn't have to read or buy the textbooks.

By next fall, my parents made me transfer to Ohio State so that I could be home with my Mother. My parents had said I had to graduate from college before I could leave home. This was a dark time for me just trying to get out of the house away from my mother. It motivated me to graduate in three years.

One day, my Dad confided in me that he had had a 'black out at work' and had to lie down on the red leather couch in his office. That weekend while mowing the back yard, he told me he fell down and almost went over the cliff and into the ravine behind our house. He had just had a check up with his doctor and was doing so well, that his blood pressure medicine was reduced by half! We had all celebrated this fact believing that it meant he would live longer. I knew nothing about health, medicine, doctors or hospitals because of my Christian Scientist background. I did not know what it meant or how to respond to what my father was telling me about his fainting and falling episodes, I could only listen.

My father was a spiritual man…an elder in his church. He prayed a lot in the morning and evening and before meals that I saw. He probably prayed a lot more than that, that I didn't see, which is the case with prayerful people. They don't flaunt or speak about their prayers. They just simply pray because it is a natural part of their living in spirit.

One morning I awoke to a scream from my mother I had never heard before or since. I got up and ran into their bedroom.

My father was still in bed which I could not understand after such a scream. She said my father was dead. He was grey in color, and I leaned over to place my hand on his face, and he was cold. I turned and walked away in shock. My Dad had stayed up with me watching TV the night before….just the two of us. We would often sit together and I would feel safe and comfortable in his energy. He would rub my arm or hand with his finger as we sat next to each other. I had gotten very tired and left him to go to bed. They said he had a massive heart attack. His heart burst during his sleep. I went into the shower and ran water over my body for a very long time and cried and cried and cried…until I thought I had no more tears left.

The world lost a fine human being that night. There were about a hundred men in black suits who flew in from all over the USA to attend his funeral. He had done many nice things for people throughout his life, and they came from everywhere to pay their respects. I knew I loved my Dad and he was a great Dad to me; but I never knew he had touched so many other people during his life. I was in shock and grief for many years. He had been my best friend…the one person in the world who would protect me. He was the first person who loved me unconditionally. The second was my grandmother who had just died.

This was the father who sat with me in a rocking chair by my bed when I was sick. Sometimes he talked to me about his work and came to see my sports games and cheered. No one else's father came to the games…only mothers. The guilt I felt at his death centered from the fact I had been feuding with him, and had not told him I loved him in the last couple of months. I know he knew I loved him, but I regretted not being nicer and more loving towards him … especially as we were fighting about the man I was intending to marry. My Dad did not like him or approve of the marriage. My Dad died before I married. I always wondered if that was because he didn't want to see it…my marriage that is.

With his death, I did not believe in God anymore. I began to center all my papers in college around death and the after life. I spent a great deal of time at the Ohio State medical library struggling to read medical books about afterlife sightings and visions documented in hospitals by doctors and nurses and administrators. I was trying to prove to myself that my father was still alive somewhere.

In my devastation over my grandmother's death and now one and one half years later, my father's, I could not see that any god would do that to a young lady who had never done anything bad in her life and tried all her life to help and heal people. Why would a loving God take the only two people in the world who loved me, who I could trust, who comforted me, away from me? My Dad was 50 when he died and I was 20.

I went into a dark place void of God and light seeking only intellectual proof through books and analyzing the spirit world and existence of God from the mind. It was not until years later studying Philosophy, and something Martin Buber wrote started to turn up that dim light in me when he said belief in God is a 'Leap of Faith', it can't be proven.

My connection and belief in God was hanging by a thread. I stayed in this dark place for years. My light inside was barely lit. I was simply angry at God and acting like a spoiled child. My understanding of the spiritual mysteries of life was limited and constricted. I was blinded by my anger and anger spawns depression. It only hurt me.

I had promised my Dad I would finish college before I got married, but I didn't think it was breaking my promise if I stayed at home and finished my degree for one semester while my new husband continued his education in another state.

Now I was left at home with my mother and brother and had just lost my grandmother and father. I had just married the young marine my Father said I could not marry and I was treading water in emotional seas. I remember when my new husband had asked my Dad for my hand in marriage and my Dad said "no".

My brother was going through his own depression of a different sort, and we were both hurting like injured animals each keeping to their own rooms and not connecting with God or each other. I knew I had to get out of the house soon and I did.

I needed to leave home. I didn't want to marry the man my Dad and Mother had picked out for me in Ohio (although we are still friends today). I didn't want that 'monied' world and class stuff I had already left in Philadelphia once. I felt it lacked substance and meaning. I wanted more from my life then money and status. Why spend your life chasing after material things at all? It was not meaningful for me.

After my father died, my mother's drinking became worse; and she returned to Chestnut Hill to be in more familiar surroundings with old friends, after I had left home to join my new husband.

me as a college girl

CHAPTER FOUR

CHESTNUT HILL WAS AN IDYLLIC SMALL village nestled in some hills outside northwestern Philadelphia, PA. It exuded charm and manners, politeness and respect for each other and all people actually. There was very little crime. We children were cloistered from all that was considered wrong and or bad in our society and the world. It was like a fairy tale for a child growing up (even with the trials I had with my mother). We were innocents.

My mother had made a lot of financial demands on my father while he was alive insisting on winter vacations in Fort Lauderdale, summers at the seashore, membership to the country club, in addition to the home in Chestnut Hill. With my Dad's passion for cars, he purchased one every year, my brother's and my private school tuitions (which was each like a college tuition both academically and financially), his inability to purchase affordable life insurance (because of his high blood pressure), and my Dad's poor money management abilities (if he had it in his pocket, he spent it) made our family relatively poor at the time of his death.

My Dad was, at the time of his death, making income in the 95 percentile of the country. But when he died, we were all dashed to the ground financially. He left the house and cars to my mother and two small life insurance policies to my brother and me. I turned mine over to my mother, because I was getting married and starting a new life and she was going to have to go back to work after not working for more then twenty years, and she asked me for it. I felt she needed the cash more then I did. I, of course, had to go to work also and vowed to never be poor again. I developed an irrational fear of becoming a 'bag lady' on the street having lived a very high life and now becoming a pauper over night.

I put my first husband through his senior year of college and three years of law school as a secretary. We chose law school for his graduate work, because, my father regretted not going to law school. I had one child with him…my only biological son. A son, whom I cherished and nurtured for many years. He was my pride and joy.

Having begun this marriage as an innocent, my eyes were opened in ways not expected by good girls of society. Even though I really didn't know what happened in their bedrooms after my friends said "I do," I was pretty sure it didn't include some of the ideas my new husband had. I lost almost all of my idealism about trust and marriage, for I also knew he was unfaithful. It was all meant to be; however, for I had to learn the experience of giving birth, motherhood, and all those accompanying joys during this marriage.

There was no spiritual growth that I could feel during this period of my life. As a matter of fact at 25 years of age I felt pushed into having my first drink. This husband was a heavy drinker like my mother. I knew the perils of alcoholism in a relationship and chose to leave it. I left with $250, a VW Bug on which I owed $600 and a small three year old child to support and care for.

Shortly after the divorce, I received a Master's of Arts degree in Philosophy, while working full- time as an administrative assistant for a hydrology grant at the University of Arizona. I had been accepted into a Ph.D. Clinical Psychology program not because I was valedictorian of my undergraduate college like the other ten people accepted into the program, but because the head of the program interviewed me and said, "you don't have the top grades, but if I needed psychological help, I would come to you ".

He was right. After only three weeks in the clinical psychology practicum course, during the first semester of the program, I was sent out to work with psychiatrists (a record for the program) and was taped and used as a 'how to do it' instruction for the rest of the students (the valedictorians). I did not want to give up this opportunity and that full ride fellowship from National Institute of Mental Health which paid me a monthly stipend for just going to school! I could support my son without working... simply going to school.

My second husband was very persuasive and manipulative and wanted us to be married. He was a rough and ready type of outdoor guy, and I learned a great deal during this second marriage about facing fear, particularly about death. I could have died repelling off a cliff in New Mexico when my husband 'forgot' to put the rope through the carrier bearings holding the sling together around my waist and hips. So when I went over the edge of the cliff, the sling flipped around and off my body. I was left hanging onto the one long fat rope next to a sheer rock cliff!

He told me to go down the rope to the bottom. The rope wasn't long enough to reach the ground, and my arms were not strong enough to hold me securely, and I would have ended up burning my hands to a bloody pulp by the time I reached the ground, so I didn't accept that suggestion. While hanging in mid-air onto this rope and dangling over a 30 foot high cliff, I said, I would try and shimmy up the rope some, and he could lean over the edge and pull me up. I had learned how to do that in gym at Germantown Friends School on rainy days when we had physical education inside. Even though we all whined about the ropes then, I was grateful for the learning experience that helped save my life.

Our fingers kept grabbing in the air and getting closer and closer until finally we connected and he pulled me up. It was surreal because while this life and death situation was progressing for his mother, my son played at the top making happy noises and having pretend adventures with small pebbles he had found. I became stronger that day obtaining more courage, perseverance, focus and determination all attributes I would need in greater and greater quantities as I proceeded with my life.

CHAPTER FIVE

MY SECOND HUSBAND WAS AN ADRENALIN junkie. Because I had been taught to please my husband, I chose to try and keep up. He not only liked adventure, he seemed at times suicidal, as I was often placed in life or death situations with him.

We used to run rivers. The Grand Colorado River as it went through Arizona from Lake Powell, to Lake Meade on the Nevada boarder was our favorite and the ultimate river to run in North America. The Little Colorado, when it hadn't rained to fill it with mud, became like the color of a swimming pool only brighter and clearer because it was from Nature. (Some say the color is caused by minerals in a spring and others say by the layer of quartzite in the river bed.). If it was that color during a trip, we played in it for hours.

The river trips were impressive, dangerous, exciting, spiritual, healing, a wilderness experience, all wrapped into one. Each Grand Canyon trip took two weeks and it was just about the only activity we enjoyed together.

My husband was known as a daredevil on the river, like running Lava Falls on the right side over the water fall or the 'hole' (20 foot in diameter water curled in and back on itself) in Crystal Rapid that would flip any size boat in a matter of a second, and wash and send the people on board (as it was overturned), down the river. He did that once, flipped, in Crystal and lost his friend for an hour. He finally found him 2 miles down river, naked and almost drown. The river had striped all his clothes off. Only his life jacket remained on his body.

For the celebration of our birthdays one year, we took a trip with our two boats and one other couple with us (4 people) on a

Colorado river trip. We camped in the inner gorge, where the river runs very deep and narrow and where if you can find a beach, it will be small (about 15 yards wide, 30 yards long) at the base of the mile high sheer rock canyon wall beside it. That night, it started to rain.

I awoke to movement under me and looked on the tent floor.... under the floor was water! I unzipped my sleeping bag, reached for the tent zipper to unzip the tent door which was zipped shut all the while trying to balance as I am riding on the floor of the tent which is washing down the beach into the river! We were able to get out and save the tent and bags and then looked for the other couple.

They were not in a flash flood but had seen what happened to us. The rain had launched spectacular waterfalls off the cliffs that plunged a third or half of a mile down the walls. We had the near miss of being washed into the Grand Colorado River inside our sleeping bags, inside our tent!

Before we could make breakfast, we heard crackling firecracker noise like lots of whips switching at once and looked up. The rain and waterfalls had loosened the rocks and we were to be at the bottom of a very big bouncing boulder rock slide. I remember looking up watching these huge boulders bouncing off the walls like rubber balls. We ran to the end of one side of the beach leaping across the gorge the water had cut in the sand where our tent had been.

The other couple ran behind some boulders that were already on the beach. At the end of the noise and boulders reaching the beach, bouncing and rolling, we looked for the other couple and walked over to them. A boulder had bounced up, after hitting another boulder on the beach, and hit the other woman in the arm breaking it. We had no doctor in sight so did the best we could ourselves with a stick and bandanas bracing her arm against any jarring movement.

A few rapids down the river was House Rock named such because there was a rock in the river that was the size of a double wide trailer. You ran this rapid to the right where 2/3rds of the river was going otherwise you went through a waterfall shoot on the left side of the rock. We headed down the tongue which is the smooth part of the river funneling down into a V shape where the speed is slow at first and then speeds up as you go down the tongue towards the point of no turning back and the waves get bigger and the noise becomes a freight train as you begin the rapid.

My husband was facing the rock with the nose of the raft but wasn't pulling fast or hard enough away from the rock to avoid it so he only had time to turn the nose to the left side of the rock and run the left side…the waterfall and shoot. We made the waterfall OK but in the tight shoot, between the rock and the slumped canyon wall, the water surges gushing over the falls and kept pushing the right side of the raft little by little up the side of House Rock until we flipped over upside down. I was sitting in the raft under water upside down in the surging water.

The rock was about 20 feet tall straight up. When I finally became untangled under the water from the ropes that held everything in the boat in case of a flip, and emerged from under the boat; I went for the big rock to get out of the rapid and avoid being caught in between the rocks with the water surging and the possibility of being sucked down in a whirlpool. How I was able to climb straight up the rock finding hand holds and foot holds and making it to the top, I don't know. I know I used a lot of adrenaline, determination and focus. You never know what you can do until you do it.

Now I was standing on top of the rock in the middle of the raging river. Everyone was looking for me in the river, and I walked across the top of the large trailer sized rock and waved to the second boatman now situated above the tongue ready to come and pick me up. All I could hear was the crashing and roar of the rapids when the water broke into the rock and continued down the river. He came down the river, reached the rock I was standing on and started pulling away from the rock underneath me, and I motioned him to come closer for my jump, but he couldn't get closer without hitting the rock which you NEVER want to do in a raging river. You could get sucked in underneath the rock or pulled down in a whirlpool which is often formed in the back wash from the river plowing into the rock, or the boat could simply get wrapped around a rock and be unable to get free as the water fills it up.

He waved for me to jump. I was afraid because he was so far away and so far below in the river (I never even liked the high diving board at the swimming pool!) I jumped and made it into the boat. Then we rescued my husband who was in the water hanging onto the side of the upside down raft fighting hypothermia.

The vastness of space and time at the Grand Canyon where the Colorado river cut down through these rocks for a mile, 1000 feet per 100,000 years, brought time into a proper perspective. Time in nature, is very different from time for human beings. You begin the Grand Canyon trip in a physical realm of awe and beauty and end in a spiritual one. It can't be helped. The majesty and beauty of Nature fills your being. The magnitude of the Canyon itself and the force and power of the river are simply overwhelming.

When you run a river, the speed, enormity and strength of the river itself leaves no room for error when rowing and maneuvering your raft. Your focus on everything surrounding you is so intense that there is no time in your life…only the river. You are in the now with no time. You move yourself into a spiritual realm, which has no time or space.

These outdoor experiences brought me close to nature again; and I started having what I call mystical experiences…when one merges with nature and loses self identity and becomes the water, the tree, etc. I would do this by first focusing on the natural object and then un-focusing my eyes on a particular spot and then with my mind pouring myself into the object as I watched say the water in a stream moving down a mountain and gurgling past wildflowers and grasses and up and over rocks along its way, having a good time as it ran down the mountainside. It is mystical. There is nothing but you and the glory of Nature.

These outdoor experiences, of course, also built confidence in me. I was very active in the community. I taught pottery at the University (without an art degree…I was just good with clay), was on a number of Boards (State, County and local) and traveled to all my son's athletic events on Fridays like my father had done for me.

CHAPTER SIX

IN 1981 I MADE MY VERY first trip to Hawaii. It was a four Island trip, and I returned most years once a year after that. It was everything I had expected and more. I would get tears in my eyes while capturing in my vision the scenic beauty of the coast lines and the many flowers and orchids growing wild in the road. The contrast of the turquoise color of the ocean against the black volcanic rock was unbelievable beauty for me to behold! I came because my father had wanted to come. The minute I saw it I knew why. It was a big turning point in my life. I felt home in Hawaii especially the next year in 1982 when I reached Molokai.

Once I stepped off the airplane in Molokai and my foot touched the asphalt runway, I expelled a deep breath from my na'au (gut) and said, "aha" as I felt peace, serenity, comfort and love. I knew I was home. At that time, I did not know that the word 'Ha' means the breath of life. I did, indeed, feel alive....finally.

During this second marriage, I traveled many countries and experienced many cultures and learned how all people throughout the world are essentially the same....all human beings. Each culture may have a slightly different twist on creation theories and what matters most in their culture, but we are all basically the same.

While on a trip to Machu Pichu, Peru, in a tiny corner store, I purchased a poster of a traditionally dressed Inca spiritual man... one view in the physical and the other in the spiritual realm. From that time in 1984 to present, that spiritual man, has been with me through my life's journey hanging on my wall along with a Hidatsu Souix Medicine Man lithograph Baskin by Leonard Baskin. These two spiritual men embody both the power and tenderness of gentle spiritual giants from differing cultures that prepared me for my future meeting of Bill Kapuni.

Souix

Spiritual Inca Man

As with my first marriage, there was a darkness of a different kind in this second marriage also. My husband was cruel, became angry and out of control for no particular reason. I became very fearful and frightened of him and finally sought out a counselor, but, in my first session, my husband tracked me down and burst into the session demanding that I leave with him. The counselor said to me as I was leaving that I should go back to school so I could support myself and my son. I applied for and was accepted to law school.

It was an exciting and joyful time of my life to be accepted to Law School! I was finally taking charge and responsibility for my own life and my own destiny. I was beginning to stand up for myself and what I wanted out of my life for me. I had never put me first before. I had always put my son first and then my husband.

I delved into the courses with exuberance. I found out I loved the law. It was logical and I knew from logic and math courses I had taken in college that I was extremely logical. I could see how the law all fit together like a giant puzzle with all the courses dovetailing together. Of course with my dyslexia, I struggled with the reading assignments. I could never finish them....only about half. Law School was much more demanding then my undergraduate or even Master's in Philosophy degree. I believe the school prided itself on flunking 1/3 of each class before graduation.

Because Law School is such a pressure cooker, you learn what everyone is about quickly, and the bonds of friendship run deep. It built confidence in me and I was able to start working out of my victim-hood.

My husband and I went through several years of marriage counseling; and my situation improved; although, I had to leave the house the last semester of school so we would not fight, for I would become distracted from my goal of graduation if we did. I moved back in after graduation, for my son's sake. I still regret leaving my son, because even though he was twelve I don't think he understood that I was doing it so he and I could have a better life. Seven days before the Bar exam, we had a fight, and I failed part of the exam by 1 point. The counselors asked me why I had moved back in. I said "for my son". When I did pass the Bar and open my solo practice, I did pro bono (free) work for battered women.

I was under a great deal of personal and family pressure to stay married. Well-bred girls didn't get divorced…no matter how bad it got (AND this would be my second failed marriage). I tried very hard for 17 years. I was so afraid at times I reached out to Spirit again. I believe people become spiritual when their surroundings are so frightening, and they have no control over their situation; that they have no one else to turn to but God, angels, ancestors, spirits. I was ready to reach out to God again because I knew I couldn't resolve my situation. I learned my first lessen in control – all you can do is control yourself no one else.

My husband stopped the fighting after I became an attorney. He might have felt my new inner strength; and since, I could no longer be intimidated by him, maybe it lost its appeal.

In addition to once again connecting with nature, and now reaching out to God, I developed a clear gift of dream prophecy. I began to have dreams that would end up as my future or someone else's future. I began to awaken the household up with my screaming 'nightmares', and then the first, non screaming dream of failing the Bar by 1 point.

CHAPTER SEVEN

At THIS TIME OF MY LIFE, I discovered that many of these prophetic dreams were to help me cope with my life and were actually a forewarning of future harm that would befall me or someone else whom I loved. They would literally and clearly precede the event or situation of the harm. At a minimum, the dreams were a signal to my psyche to get ready for something. The dreams went so far as to give me slow motion time frames before the circumstances would happen in reality. I would also have a great deal of déjà vu. Déjà vu is what people experience when they think that they have lived this moment or moments before and instantaneously know what is coming next. Having a lot of déjà vu is often the beginning of opening to psychic awareness of what I call the force, spirit, or life flow; because I believe it is a connection to the difference in the concept of time in this physical world and the 'no time' in the world of Spirit.

Other forms of awakening to know you are connected to a 'life flow' can for example be when you are thinking of someone and they call, or you are thinking of someone and you see them in town or they call or write you. This means you are connected in the world of Spirit.

My biological son, was a junior in High School. He was playing varsity football, had good grades, didn't drink, or smoke and was a peer helper at the school, one who is elected to be the listener if anyone is having trouble. I was very proud that he seemed to be following in my footsteps on a Spiritual path. He showed a deep level of empathy for others and was happy to give comfort and direction to others in distress.

One night I had a vivid dream about a car accident. It was at night, I was 'floating' behind the driver that I did not know and looking through the windshield when the car lights from the on coming traffic became very bright and came towards the car I was in. Lights flashed bright in the huge shape of a star found in the comic books, and I awoke screaming. I was shaken. I didn't understand.

I told my husband and my son about it because I woke them up. Some time later within a few weeks, I had the dream again only I could see more detail. I knew it was a male driving, I saw pine trees, and the road looked like it was in the mountains at night. I heard the sound of the crash. This time I was frightened, and I cautioned us all to drive with extreme care...thinking that could change the future.

The third time I had the dream a few weeks later, I was sitting in the middle of the back seat, and felt someone beside me but didn't know who it was; and I saw the crash at night in the mountains and this time I saw it was my son driving! Everything went black with the crash...all there was... were my screams. I demanded that my son not drive at night and not drive in the mountains and not drive with anyone in the back seat. He agreed....again I was thinking this would change the future. It wasn't until much later when I connected to a Native American Medicine Man that I learned which of my dreams I could change and which I could not.

On Valentines' day, I wasn't feeling very well so I stayed in bed while my husband left for work and my son took off for school with the rose, that he showed me the night before, he had bought for his girl friend for school the next day. I got out of bed and started walking for the door entering the hall, when my head was jerked backward so violently that I had to grab onto the door frame to keep from falling over backwards. I gathered myself together and went down the hall and saw the back of my son walking away from me. He was in such detail and so real that I called to him and asked him why he was home? There was no answer and he disappeared 'into thin air'. I was confused but now know, he was saying goodbye to me.

I made it into the kitchen and thought I should look at the clock to see what time it was because something 'strange was happening'. It was 7:30 am. I put some hot water on in the kettle for my oatmeal and coffee and went back to the bathroom to take my shower before getting ready to go to work. While in the shower the phone rang. I grabbed a towel and caught the phone. It was the sheriff who asked me if I owned a VW bug giving the color and year. I said, "yes". He said there has been an accident and your son and another boy were in the car. I said, "no, it's not my son, he went to school alone". He replied, "they are at the hospital".

I hung up and started screaming and getting dressed. Then, I stopped immediately. I was not going to accept into my reality any negative thoughts about my son. Then, got into the pickup and started speeding down the dirt road and towards the hospital. I ran into the emergency doors and was stopped from going into the ER patient area. I saw a doctor friend of mine and told him what had happened and that my son was in there, and I needed to see him. He went in and came out and said, "Ok, you can go in, he is in very bad shape and he will look terrible".

I ran in and saw him lying on a cold steel table without his sweater or shirt on and a neck brace on and across his nose was a bandage, which was being used to hold his nose on his face. His head was split from the tip of his nose to the back of his head and a kotex was stuffed in the split. I went up to his head and spoke in his ear while touching and rubbing his shoulder and said, "How you 'doin', honey"? With that he did a sit up on the table....because of football training, I suppose, and being in excellent shape. He said, "I want to go home".

The circle of doctors and nurses gave a sigh of relief and some clapped because they thought he had died. He actually did, and came back. I asked that he be covered, because the steel was cold. Arrangements were immediately made to transport him to Fort Collins because the Laramie hospital was too small for a patient who had his skull cracked open, and had a heart attack when his chest was crushed by the truck that had run over his VW and had his face and head cut open.

I called my doctor in Fort Collins and told him what had happened. He said he would get all the doctors I needed there and have them waiting for us when we arrive. We took an ambulance instead of a helicopter because my son was critically injured. He vomited during the trip down-- a sign of severe brain injury. We got there and the three doctors promised me were there waiting at the Emergency doors. The plastic surgeon excused himself saying we had much more important matters to tend to before we would be needing him. Then the heart doctor left after he felt my son was stable, and then I was left with two neurosurgeons and given books on brain damage to read.

I glanced over them, but all the while from the time when the sheriff called, I prayed and never once accepted that there was an injury or that my son would die. I refused to accept that reality. I never let it cross my mind. I kept praying; and I even, while we were separated for the short time he had a cat scan, looked out the window and had the audacity to make a deal with God. Although I had been reaching out to Spirit during my horrible marriage, I was not quite back to my state of believing. I said, "if he lives, I promise you I will try and believe in you again."

I never left my son for 31 hours straight. I watched them pick out the bone chips that came from his skull in the gaping head wound and replace the kotex with bandages on top. The top of his head had swollen to the width and depth, and length of the Kotex pad on its side. I watched them sow his nose back on to his face, as I talked to him and rubbed his arm or shoulder. I went to intensive care with him and talked to him all the while.

At that time, I was only allowed in 15 minutes every hour in ICU. I sat and simply prayed the other 45 minutes of each hour outside his room. I went in at the exact time every hour all the while talking to him and rubbing his shoulder and arms and hands. The words I was saying were important I discovered later on, because I was doing visual imagery with him and his brain saying such things as when you travel along this road in your brain and it is bombed out, just build a bridge or go around that area and find a way back to the main road. Instinctively (or with spiritual guidance) I was teaching him to rebuild and readjust his brain neuro-pathways to circumvent any blocks or destroyed areas.

The doctors had told me he had significant brain damage determined from the cat scan. He was missing whole areas of his brain function now; but I knew we only used 10% of our brain matter, and that there would be more he could tap into and use. I already knew he was in bad shape mentally because when I asked him to move his finger, if he could hear me, I waited a full minute before he moved -- his arm. He had to go around a lot of bombed out areas!

I told him to "be a road builder and road engineer and construct new highways to use traveling through" his brain. When I was 'working on him' (today I would say healing him), I placed my hand on his head and felt like I was Dr. Spock from Star Trek in a mind melding session like was done in the TV series. But I was giving him light energy from above, for I was to later learn I was a conduit for healing energy.

The next afternoon the nurses finally talked me into leaving for a while and taking a nap. I missed a couple hours, and the first hour I missed coming into the ER for my fifteen minute interval, my son who had been in a coma, sat up, took off his oxygen mask, took off his heart monitors, took out his IV, got out of bed and started walking down the hall looking for me. The nurse told me what he had done. He said when I asked him where he was going, "Looking for you!" When he came out of his coma, the first thing he said was: "I am an only child". I interpreted that to mean that he knew he had to survive for me.

I took him home after 4 days and the nurses said, "It was a miracle. Most people who come in with this much damage are here three months". The doctors told me not to expect much from him mentally. Certainly he couldn't go to college now because he had so much brain burned out, and he may even have trouble with some of his courses in high school. If so, I was told to just take him out of that course and put him into something easier. They told me not to let him get frustrated.

After he went home, and for a few weeks, he had to concentrate on how to walk. I walked behind him with my hands on his shoulders and said right foot, left foot…. At home, I had to start him out reading comic books and used flash cards to bring back addition and subtraction! He ultimately went on to college earned a BS degree in Electrical Engineering and a Masters and PhD. in Material Science Engineering. I never told him what the doctors had said!

At home, I saw the police report. The accident was at 7:30 AM. Pine trees lined the street, and a pine tree branch obscured the visibility of the stop sign he ran when he was hit by the raised big tired 4-wheel drive truck. The venipane of the VW had been pushed into him from his nose up his face to the top of his head. That is what cut him open. The VW seat had jumped its runners and faced the truck as it ran over him and crushed his chest. If the seat had not jumped I was told he would have been crushed to death by the truck. I was told it took the EMTs 45 minutes to cut the metal and get him out of his car. His friend was riding in the back seat and received no injuries.

It was a miracle healing with God, prayer, energy, and positive affirmations. It was a miracle he survived the crash, he came back from the dead, his brain didn't swell, and he was able to work around the burned out portions of his brain. I came back to God. I would not have been able to live with just my husband absent the only joy in my life at that time, my son. God knew that too.

Interestingly enough, a little more then a week went by and another young man in the same neighborhood was in a car crash on the interstate and suffered brain damage and was in a coma also. I called up the parents and told them what I had done when my son was in a coma with brain damage… talked to him and touched him and gave him positive statements and prayed. They told me they sat outside the room. Their son died.

CHAPTER EIGHT

MY SON WENT BACK TO PLAYING sports; and, in the late summer during football camp of his senior year of High School, he came home and told me one of his coaches wanted as many people from the team as possible to go to the Tony Robins fire walk in Colorado. "The University of Hawaii football team had done it!", he said.

My son wanted to do it. I didn't want him to. I thought it would be too dangerous, but he was a senior and after the 3rd time he asked me, I said, "OK, but I'm going to make sure you'll be all right. I'll go with you, but I won't walk".

We drove down to Colorado on a Friday afternoon after school let out. About 200-300 people attended. We all went out to see the giant logs that would be burned for our coals in our walk.

Tony Robbins was a very positive motivational speaker. After what seemed like a very short time we all went outside where a fire walk of about 20 yards long had been made in the parking lot by a path of burning embers like what is in the bottom of your fireplaces after they have been burning for a few hours the glowing orange color appears. Men would shovel the glowing embers out onto the path. We had learned a chant in the large room inside, and each person who began to walk was started in the chant before you started walking; and you were reminded to keep your eyes looking up at a 45 degree angle at all times during the walk.

My son was the first person to go through! I watched him in amazement. I was near the end of the line and still unsure whether I would walk or not when my son came up to me and said I would.

I remember his eyes. They were bright, alive and had white flecks around the pupils. He was in Spirit.

A few of us parents had come to protect our children, but they were already through the walk and we were sort of ringing our hands wondering if we should, could or would go as we moved towards the front of the line. All of a sudden I was there, started my chant and lifted my eyes towards the stars. I remember the first few steps. I felt no heat, but I felt the bumps of the coals under my feet. These were fresh orange yellow coals that had just been placed out.

There was no time during the walk. I have no idea how long it was. Peripherally, I saw the people gathered around, heard the drums pounding, and could see the orange yellow path ahead of me as I was walking; and soon I was aware I was near the end. When I dropped my focus from the stars and stopped my chant as I pulled my left foot (toes) off the coals (the right foot was already on a pad of grass sod), I looked straight at the people who were pulling me off with my arm and one was pulling my left foot off the coals. Almost the instant I stopped looking up and looked at the person, I felt the heat on my toes! This was an extremely high spiritual experience. You had to be so high you couldn't feel the heat from the coals. If you couldn't experience and feel the heat, it wasn't burning and it wasn't occurring.

I had charcoal smudges on my feet, and I remember I didn't wash my feet. I let it wear off. It was like a badge of honor for what I had been able to do. The people who didn't walk or who let their fear overtake their intentions were soaking their feet in a kiddy pool of ice cold water.

My husband was on a sabbatical leave from the University for six months and had come home for a surprise visit the evening of the fire walk. I had already ended our relationship in my heart; because I had had a cancer scare, and he had refused to go with me for the tests —choosing to meet his graduate student in the field instead. With my charcoal smudged feet and law degree, I filed for divorce and reclaimed my life.

CHAPTER NINE

I MOVED TO DENVER TO TRY life a new and on my own. I poured myself into my work working as much as 70 hours per week and my wolf dog was suffering at home in my condo alone. One Sunday I looked out my window and saw a boy, his grandfather and what appeared to be the boy's father playing tennis. I thought they needed a fourth so I got on my tennis shoes and grabbed my racket to go out and join them.

We met and played a while. It was exercise and company of which I had none, and the man seemed very nice. He worked at home out of his condo and offered to take care of my dog during the day.

He also was coming off a divorce and was afraid of relationships and marriage like I. We became very good friends, attending CU sports events and dining out together once in a while. The Colorado Buffalos were hot in those days going to the Orange bowl two times. Our common interests were the Buffalos, my dog and Indian culture.

My interest in Native Americans began in my previous marriage when we had traveled to New Mexico often, and I learned about Indian culture as I learned the ways of New Mexico pueblo potters at Santa Clara and San Eldefonzo. This man knew a lot about Indian culture having been on Rosebud reservation during the Russel Means and Dennis Banks turbulent times. He had been an investigator on a murder case on the reservation that was made into a movie called Thunderheart.

Very similar to Hawaiians, Indians are true naturalists and lovers of Nature. They believe there is a kinship with all creatures of the earth, sky and water. Indigenous peoples feel safe among the creatures of the earth and there exists a brotherly feeling where often they speak a common tongue. Their culture knows that man's heart away from nature becomes hard; which leads to the lack of respect for growing and living things, which soon leads to lack of respect for humans also. Keeping close to nature keeps a softening influence on the heart.

After three years of friendship, we married. I thought it would be my last marriage because we hardly ever fought and seemed to be very compatible. It was a bad sign perhaps when he got in another car to leave the wedding without me.

We moved from Denver to Arizona because he had a new job, one of many as I would soon find out. He had difficulty staying in one place for very long. I liked Arizona because we would be close to my son who was now doing graduate work at the U of A in Tucson. We saw my son several times a month and built a lovely retirement home in north Scottsdale. My mother moved south of Tucson and my brother came West to live with us for a while. This was the closest my family members had ever lived together and it was some of our best 'family' times. I was calm and peaceful as all of us were happy.

Then after a few years, he got the wanderlust and decided it was time for him to move to New Mexico. He moved for a new job and left me to fix up the house and sell it and move us to Albuquerque. I was not happy about the move at all. He had promised me Scottsdale would be the last move as he now promised this move to Albuquerque would be the last move. I am not a rolling stone. I bloom where I am planted and did not like to be yanked out by the roots again.

The positive thing is I took up pottery again and once again being in New Mexico the home of more Indian tribes than any other state, I became immersed in that culture once more. It was very natural to me, and I did love the light spiritual energy I felt in New Mexico. This was to be my place of quantum spiritual growth.

After looking at more then 100 homes, my husband and I chose to live in the south east foothills of the city; where the US Air Force, literally had the top of a mountain open up and helicopters would descend, James Bond like, within the mountain out of sight. This was the area of the country where we have a great underground railway system carrying missiles with warheads on flatbeds to move them around so that Russia could not obliterate all the US missiles at once.

It was a marvelous house. An engineer built it for his wife. It was very large and had spacious rooms (many of them) and a large back and front yard I would soon turn into splendid gardens. I had a special daylily garden and a special rose garden, both of which gave me great pleasure as I sat out in the back yard.

I soon moved from a pottery workspace I had been renting to home, because I was inspired to create 'spirit vessels." These were sculpted pieces that I literally felt guided to create. I knew somehow they were important, and I prayed before making them because I felt energy move through me into them. I can only say they were made through me not by me. In all I made over 200 of them and they went all over the world to people who saw them at art shows. Each piece was one of a kind, unique.

They ranged in size from one to four feet high. The first two I made were more like vases instead of people, but had energy in them nevertheless. Most of them after that had faces on them. The ones who did not I was told, by Black Raven, "did not want to be seen." I made the faces without any purpose or intention of what I was doing and with no art in sculpture instruction. I simply sat down with a lump of clay and pretty soon within an hour, there was a face that appeared, and then I hollowed out the head so I could apply it to the slabs of clay I had rolled and assembled.

At first I rolled out the slabs of clay like I did when baking a pie crust. I used a rolling pin. I was a purest with clay. Everything had to be hand made with the exception of using a wheel for throwing pots. But eventually I used a slab rolling machine similar to the old fashioned ringers on washing machines. I had developed a purist attitude in the 70's when watching the Indian potters make their beautiful pottery with coils and gourds scraping the walls to make the walls smooth and uniform. It was a spiritual act working only with the hands and handmade tools.

I prayed and purified myself each time before I made the slabs. I found that I had to keep meditating and praying when I made the slabs; because early on I would feel the energy surge through my body and arms and hands near the completion of a sculpture. After a while, I was trusted and the energy began to enter the clay at the time I rolled the slabs.

The slabs were made in a particular order and carried on top of one another usually two or three at a time with plastic in between so that they wouldn't stick together. I would carry them to the car like a child in my arms. I always thought of them as my children and spoke of them as my children.

What was amazing was that as I rolled the pieces out and stacked them, they remained in their stacked position and were used with the piece laying next to them in the creation of a vessel. They were already planned to be together in a certain way. Some of them fit together even though the laws of physics would say they shouldn't be able to, and some clay people asked me what kind of clay I used, what did I put in it to make it stay the way I formed it? The pieces were made of ordinary stoneware wheel throwing clay but performed outside of their normal physical limitations because of what they were.

Most when assembled had Indian faces who, in the beginning, looked like a family because the facial features looked somewhat similar. What amazed me was that the vessels sold in the order in which they were made! Zuni Indian Nation was considered among pueblo Indian tribes to be the most spiritually evolved. The creation of the vessels connected me to one of the very important medicine men in Zuni, an elder called Black Raven.

Black Raven was a man of eighty something years of age. He lived in a Hogan in Zuni land 10 miles from a trading post. He had neither a car nor a horse, but simply walked. Mostly he stayed at his Hogan by himself.

My husband had met him a long time ago, when my father-in-law was one of the founders of the Native American Rights Foundation in Boulder Colorado a number of years prior. The Zunis were the first tribe to use the US legal system against the US government and Bureau of Indian Affairs (BIA.) My husband had become a son of the Sioux Nation in South Dakota, betrothed to an Indian maiden, and went on his spirit quest and lived among the Indians there for a while. Because of all this, he knew many chiefs and medicine men in various tribes. Zuni was in New Mexico and he would be in contact with Black Raven on occasion. As I continued down my spiritual path more and more often they would talk about me, because Black Raven began having visions about me and the vessels.

One of my First Spirit Vessels

I had visited many reservations, historical ruins and kivas and wanted to visit the ones south of Albuquerque, which were the ruins of places where the Spanish had enslaved the Indians to build Missions and Catholic Churches. I never had fear of the unknown energies I felt, particularly of Indians, who I knew through their culture; and I did not expect the dark energy I felt. Perhaps, the spirits resented their slavery by Spainards (whites) still yet.

I am a person of light and I walk with an open heart and open spiritual chakras. With this incident, I learned one must protect themselves if they walk between the worlds as I do. I had to learn how to filter my chakras from dark energies. I sat down on the edge of a Kiva with my legs dangling over the side and felt a presence beside me. I did not mind it except, it entered into my body through my ear and began talking to me.

I became frightened and called out to my husband who came running to me, because of the fear he heard in my voice. He came and intuitively jumped in the space next to where I was sitting and helped me up. I was unaware of what had happened, but he said my voice was exceedingly slow for some time as the residual energy of the intruder remained.

We went to the car and I put the car in the wrong gear and it lurched forward instead of backwards. I then drove us to the nearest town which was quite small and stopped the car (I thought I was stopping the car, but it ran into a wall instead of stopping). We got out and went inside an old store with large front windows and the gold painted writing on them for something to drink and eat. I gave my husband the keys. All the way home, I was in a daze and confused as to what had happened and wanted to call an Indian friend of mine who had been a client in Denver.

Upon reaching home I did call and was given a chant to memorize and say for protection. I began saying the chant, but still feeling "odd", I simply rested. They told me I had been psychically attacked. It was Sunday.

Monday my husband got in touch with Black Raven and found out what had happened. In Indian culture, there is no good or bad there simply is. Black Raven said the being that attacked me was only mischievous, but warned me to never go back there again. Black Raven also told my husband it is rare for someone to come out of an attack like that so quickly if at all, and that by my strong mind, my husband's intuition to jump into the intruder's space coupled with his love and sense of protection for me was what drove off the intruder.

CHAPTER TEN

BLACK RAVEN KNEW ABOUT WHEN I started to make the spirit vessels. He saw me in visions and saw what I was doing and who I was helping by doing it. Apparently the beings I was bringing into this reality were coming back to help prevent something from happening or assist someone here already facing harm. The Spirit vessel would help that person and there was only one person for each vessel. That is why I couldn't sell the vessels to people who were not meant to have them. So I stopped trying to sell them at all. The people who were meant to have them found them on their own sometimes crying sometimes yelling when they somehow recognized the vessel to belong to them.

He said that he had never known of a white person being chosen to do this type of work and pressed on questioning my husband further about me. Apparently, because I was raised a Christian Scientist (and he had read the Science and Health with Key to the Scriptures) which is not unlike Native beliefs and not a traditional "Christian/Judeo" religion; I was able to transcend those religious Christian/Judeo beliefs and understand and comprehend the other realities recognized by indigenous cultural peoples throughout the world. I was chosen because of my purity and unique spiritual orientation to do this work.

This was all confirmed by two people who purchased some vessels and took them to psychics to find out more about them. The beings, Black Raven said, were from the fifth dimension, and the psychics independently concurred. I was chosen to birth them here so they could help certain people and the psychics said I needed to be thanked for bringing them here. I felt it was meant to be, so that

I could learn more of the spirit world, life flow, and God sufficiently so that I would be a closer equal to Bill Kapuni when I eventually met him.

After this attack, Black Raven told my husband I needed to go to water to purify myself. There is not a lot of water in New Mexico only a few lakes and streams. I chose a body of water north of Santa Fe, and we drove to Nambe Pueblo. I walked back through their lands to the falls where there is a three tier water fall from the spill way of a dam built to the top of the ridge. I went into spirit by praying and meditating as I walked in the stream back to the falls. There is a tight spot to walk in between the rocks, and when you come out, it opens up and there are the falls. The water is cold and the sound is rushing.

In the farthest back pool there is a small sandy beach where I walked and sat on a rock and meditated. I would open my eyes every once in a while to see the rocks and look at their many faces. There were so many faces on the rocks there! Like guardians of the pools. I studied their faces when my eyes were open.

At some point I decided to walk into the cold pool little by little. I had waited until all people were gone. There were hardly any people there most times I went. Some days there were Indians who would sit and watch me go in. Apparently I would stand to almost my waist in this freezing water for very long periods of time. No one else would even enter. I would stand with my arms stretched out from my body in the form of giving homage and praying and meditating with my eyes closed just listening to the sound of the falls and feeling the water all around me and being in spirit.

This first time, to purify from the attack, was unique because I had a very powerful and strong vision. As I raised my arms to the sky, a shaft of light surged through the earth through the water through my body and straight up to the universe. As I turned my face upward in prayer, the light opened my eyes and poured through my eyes to the heavens, like I was a shell where the light consumed the inside of me and poured out through my eye sockets towards the universe and beyond.

I knew something had happened to me. Obviously I was purified by the water and light. My husband said I was in the freezing water for 40 minutes. I never felt the cold, but because I focus on eyes as the window to the soul, when I got into the car, I looked in the mirror at my eyes. They were amazing! The color around the pupils had changed to white spikes so that the pupil area looked like stars with a black center. I just kept looking at my eyes in the mirror on the way home not believing the change.

CHAPTER ELEVEN

Early on, in the second batch of vessels, I made a total of four vessels that were not made apparently through light. After they were made, I could feel their dark energy. They were not like the others. My husband called Black Raven to tell him of the experiences we were having like confusion and forgetting things and quarreling (which we never did). Black Raven said the dark energies saw what I was doing and wanted to come through also. There were a total of four dark energy beings who came through me into the clay and needed now to be contained. They came because I needed to learn about and experience this dark energy; because I had always seen light, not darkness, in people throughout my whole life.

Black Raven instructed my husband to take the first two vessels back to the area close to where I had been attacked but not exactly at that specific place. He followed the instructions to this new place, and left them on a family's land. Apparently, according to Black Raven, these two vessels wanted to be close to their family. It had been difficult to get them into the car. There was a lot of mental interference from them even though they were filled inside with charcoal which rendered them less powerful. Charcoal absorbs negative energy, contains it and renders it powerless.

Black Raven told us to take the remaining two to the mountains off a lonely road where they would not be in contact with any people. This was surprisingly difficult. We were planning a driving trip to Arizona to see my son and mother. We looked at the map and saw where we could travel a route through lonely mountains. I was to pick my husband up at work at noon. At 1:00 pm I was still trying to get out of the house!

Even though the two vessels were outside facing away from the house and to the north, which rendered them less powerful, and filled with charcoal, I encountered lots of mental interference in getting clothes organized and out to pack, in packing the suitcase, in even getting it zipped up, in getting out the door into the car, in catching my ghost beads on a drawer that was pulled out and they caught on the corner and broke spattering all the beads all over the kitchen floor. I had to pick up all the beads. How the drawer was left open and how I happened to bend down close to it and pull up catching the strand on the corner is beyond me.

Indian ghost beads are made with pinion seeds. They are gathered by Indian children. The squirrels bite off one end and the other end is cut. Then there is an open tunnel that runs through the seed and they are sewn into a necklace. The ghost beads are made by Indians for protection from dark spirits. During this time with these dark vessels in and around our house, I even placed Indian ghost beads around the necks of our three dogs instead of collars.

My husband called the house to see where I was. I was breathless. I finally got the vessels into the trunk and covered them up so they couldn't see where they were going. After I picked him up, we were off on our five hour drive with a short detour into the mountains. Black Raven also told us that as long as the vessels are not chipped, the spirit is trapped inside. Once they enter the vessel they can not escape without the vessel breaking.

I was able to take the first vessel back in the forest far off the trail. When the second vessel was being created, it had not allowed any slip to be painted over its' eyes in readiness for firing in the kiln (the slip would move away from the eyes every time they were painted.) When I walked this second vessel back into the forest along a dirt ridge, I tripped and fell against a tree breaking a chip off the vessel. I quickly picked it up and put it inside the vessel already full of charcoal. I had to focus as hard as I could to just be able to drop it off in the woods so no one would come upon it. It was very difficult because I was bumping into the trees with my shoulders as I went along even though it had chipped.

I did it and as we left the area I could feel that the car was free of the black energy. It was as if a great weight was off my back and shoulders when I was outside their sphere of influence. I knew I would have to purify again when we got home because I had held them and mentally fought them off.

CHAPTER TWELVE

I STOPPED MAKING THEM FOR A while after experiencing those four dark energies in the house; only the line of the 5th dimension energies was forming to come through and getting backed up again. After feeling for several days pressure to make more, I began to notice small little lights in the back yard. They were like the white tiny Christmas lights, but they were not white. They were a pale apricot color. I tried to figure out where they were coming from and searched the back yard for the source of the lights-- nothing. My husband had seen them and watched our dog play with them and roll in the grass while they would bounce off her. I realized it was the beings again wanting to come into this world. I started up again with the process.

I had breakage of a few vessels during a show when vinyl blew into my booth and knocked three vessels over. Black Raven had seen this in a vision. He knew each vessel very well, and saw in his visions what they were coming here to do.

My work was shown and sold now in six galleries in four states. Black Raven had said to keep the price down on the vessels because people who needed them might not be able to afford them if I did not, so I did.

At the first show it seemed that the people who purchased them were people predominantly in the health fields. Then there was a show when people in wheelchairs came to get their vessels. During these early shows, somehow the faces resembled the persons buying them, which I thought was uncanny. People wrote me to send me pictures of their piece in their home and tell me what they named it. It was such an exciting time for me to think I had a gift that was being used for a good purpose and the people getting their vessels were excited and energized. I felt good about my purpose in life.

While I was preparing for that first show and not realizing what or how important these pieces really were, I remember I had them all on and around the table in the family room. I left the kitchen to go into the family room, because I heard so many people talking a language I did not understand and thought I had left the TV on; and I was going to turn it off. No one was there and there was no TV on. As soon as I entered the room, the talking stopped.

During the middle time of creating vessels and after the dark energy came through, and was taken care of, I was awakened two consecutive nights by strange beings, and my husband had to call Black Raven again to find out what was happening. The first night was a being the size of myself at the corner of the bed. I was awakened and although scared, walked through it to go to the bathroom. It disappeared when I walked through it. The second night I was awakened by an extremely tall one that came up through the bed between my husband and I and touched the 10 foot ceiling we had. There were two others that accompanied this large one at the foot of the bed and by the TV.

They were tall, relatively thin, and cylindrical shapes (like telephone poles) that had a dark grayish-black cloth draped around them. The cloth was made of narrow triangles back to back so that two of them together appeared to look like a diamond shape on its side. They reminded me of the chain links on the armor the knights in the middle ages wore only larger. They were very flexible. It was not shiny but like dull grey metal and the color of pewter.

One of the beings opened the 'blanket' and underneath was an iridescent neon green body of simply tubes about four inches in diameter similar to the pipe cleaner men I used to make with my Dad's pipe cleaners. I became afraid again and got up and walked into the bathroom. They immediately disappeared and never returned again.

They had no ears no mouth but huge eyes. It was almost like they had four eyes in each place there was to be an eye. That is why I changed the eyes on the faces from that point on. I couldn't put four eyes on the faces, but I made their eyes deeper and to have four pupils like having four eyes, and there eyes then looked like they had stars in them. I made them more like the beings I saw.

After hearing the description of these beings from my husband, Black Raven said they were the fifth dimensional beings coming through me and were just coming to check on the progress I was making. The blankets enabled me to see them he said. I was far too surprised and afraid to acknowledge them, although I wish I had now. Fear is a debilitating emotion for us. At the time, everything was terribly overwhelming for me. Early on, before Black Raven was in my life and I started this path, I was wondering if I was going crazy. I wasn't. I was just experiencing quantum spiritual growth. I believe I was learning new spiritual knowledge from the beings going through my body and I began to acknowledge my own gifts. That's why he stayed in contact with my husband so much, and guided me. He kept me grounded in this reality.

CHAPTER THIRTEEN

I BELIEVE THE DARK ENERGY CAME through me in the four vessels to teach me about dark energy and how to protect myself. I needed to stay in light and spirit at all times working in clay, and all times period. I couldn't get angry or upset about anything while working with any part of the vessels. I was learning about powers and energies outside our physical realm and soon recognized my own ability to transfer energy. This was a new way I began to heal. Most of this was all good as I was beginning to heal people, but on two occasions, I used my ability in anger instead of light and love. I now believe, negative emotions like hate and anger, attract darkness into your life in the form of negative people, situations, illness or dark energy; and when you use your God given gifts for a negative purpose, it will come back on you.

I was at a football game where the lady in front of me kept banging into my knee with her chair, which she was rocking back and forth hitting my knee every time she came back. My knee was beginning to hurt now. I leaned over to my husband and told him I was going to give her back all the hurt she had caused in my knee. I did it with my mind's vision transferring the energy through my knee to her back. Pretty soon, she began to start rubbing her back. I looked at him. Then she rubbed it more and more and moved forward to rub it with both hands. Then suddenly, she stood up and grabbed the chair and gave it away to someone else on her row.

I didn't think that was such a bad thing to do, give back the hurt someone gave me (like the Old Testament in the Bible teaches – "an eye for an eye"). I now understand that because my intentions were to hurt her, I was using dark energy, which would attract negative energy back to me; and I would be the one to suffer.

The second and last time, I used my gifts in anger or 'pay back time' was in a parking lot close to where we lived. I had driven there to order and pick up a pizza and taken Maggie, my Welsh Springer (like a cocker spaniel only longer body and bigger) with me. When I came out with the pizza, she somehow got out of the car, when I put the pizza in the car, and she was walking around the car to a white pickup truck that had pulled up right next to me. Why next to me I don't know because there were plenty of spaces all around. Maggie went around to his truck to sniff the tires as dogs do and he got out and tried to kick her! I said, "Don't kick my dog".

He grumbled about her walking around in the parking lot. I put her back in the car and then leaned against the side of my car and folded my arms across my chest. He kept grumbling and I said, "you don't kick a dog". Clouds had gathered over the parking lot now. I heard thunder in the distance and raised my right arm and pointed to the sky in anger and pointed to the clouds.

At that moment, a streak of lightening came out of the clouds down towards the parking lot and the man ran to and did jump into his truck and took off like a bat out of H---. I turned around and saw a small group of people who had come out of the pizza place and watched what was happening in the parking lot and now were talking to each other and pointing to the clouds and me. They had obviously seen what had happened. This was my second and last time I ever used any gift I might have been given in anger. I left not wanting to talk to anyone from the small crowd that had gathered afraid they might talk to me about what had happened. I didn't understand it myself yet. My intention was to teach this guy a lesson about kicking dogs, and the result was swift and powerful. Dark energy works instantaneously.

CHAPTER FOURTEEN

I KNEW BLACK RAVEN THROUGH MY husband, but never really met him in person; as I was a white woman. Black Raven trusted and used my husband to read and write letters and speak with white people for him. He knew me in spirit and I him. I soon realized that black ravens were usually around me, at home, outside, at shows, and particularly driving to and from shows while I was in the car. They would fly along the side of the car, sometimes looking at me as they were level with my window, but mostly flying overhead either over the car or out a ways to the side of the road. On a few trips during long straight stretches of road they would be flying with me and criss-crossed the road over the car.

I first noticed black ravens in connection with my work when I had the garage door open. The garage was my studio, and they would fly over the driveway and over the garage periodically. Once when a friend of mine, was visiting me and we drove out to visit a pueblo, I told her how ravens follow me in the car. She was skeptical. We pulled off the main road to a dirt road for a stop and a huge black raven that had been flying near the car followed us off the road and sat on top of a fence post right next to my car door and looked at me. She looked at the raven and at me, smiled and said "OK, I believe you."

When Black Raven died I cried even though I had never met him. He chose his time and place to die as spiritual leaders at his level often do. He had his daughter drive him to a hill where his wife was buried and asked her to go back to the truck and get a blanket. When she returned with the blanket, he had died lying on the ground next to his wife.

I was greatly saddened because he had been my guide during this portion of my spiritual growth in New Mexico and I felt I knew him. I did know him in spirit.

I drove out to the Albuquerque Indian Cultural Center one day and coincidentally the Zunis were to dance that day. I saw them and approached them to talk about Black Raven in my sorrow. The lead dancer told me not to be sad, because Black Raven watched over me here in this world, he would always watch over me. As he looked at the space over my left shoulder, he said, "he is here with you now".

We continued talking and I told him how much I enjoyed Pow Wow which I attended every year in April at the University of New Mexico basketball arena for the Gathering of Nations. It is the largest Pow Wow in the world where more then a thousand dancers (both fancy and traditional) and drummers gather to compete and dance.

He immediately said, "Dance with us today". I shook my head all right. In a few moments, they placed me right behind the lead dancer, who was at the head of the line going into the circle. Within a few seconds, I was in Spirit. It was one of the most wonderful experiences in my life. They then encircled me and wove their line around me as they danced, I looked up to the sky and a large black raven flew over us! I don't know how long we danced. When you are in Spirit, there is no time.

One Sunday after Black Raven died, I was feeling particularly down and my husband said we need to go to Zuni, for he had been told there was a black raven talisman in a circular case there for me. We drove out and as always I felt better just being on that reservation. We went into the trading post and started looking at all the ravens carved out of stone. I didn't see any for me, but finally near the end of the circled line of cases I saw the black raven. As I looked at it, it raised up towards me. It was indeed in an elliptical case. It was the only round case in the trading post. From that time on, I have carried it with me always until a few years ago.

I believe when we enter this physical world, we are given several options to exit. In other words, we have choices as to when we leave this reality and move on. Maybe it is something like we have dropped out of a course at college because it seems too hard for us, or we have learned enough. All I am sure of at this point in my life learning process is that the life force is a mystery and far too complicated to understand from this physical world. All we can each do is push forward on a path of light towards God.

I do believe, however, we come here to learn about and deal with at least four concerns: fear, love, control and money. If we were in school I would say these are our four degree subject areas to study. While we are in these schools of learning, we are on our spiritual paths and grow spiritually through all our experiences.

During the time of making the vessels, I was mostly living in spirit and when you do that there is no time. There is only now. After I misused my gifts during the middle of my years making the vessels, but after Black Raven died, I was once again attacked only this time physically on a spiritual level. Everyday I sat in the lazy boy unable to do anything, paralyzed by pain in my left shoulder. Every morning before my husband left for work, he would work on my back (he had been trained in massage) and pop my shoulder back in place. Somehow not doing anything, just sitting there in the chair, it would simply pop out again.

I was getting tired of the pain and inability to do anything. Finally I started to have a dream about it. I saw Black Raven in my dream who told me I could take care of it myself and to turn around and look at my back, only I couldn't see my back. In the second dream I was able to turn around and see my back. There was a hideous black creature with long talons digging into my shoulder. It was about a foot long looking like a gargoyle on the medieval buildings. Now with Black Raven and my dream, I knew what was wrong I just had to figure out how to get rid of it. He told me I would be able to.

I sat there and in my ways of prayer, light, meditation, smudging (burning sage) relaxation, I still received no relief or healing. I sat and thought and thought and prayed for an answer. All of a sudden I got the white sage which I had already been using to purify myself and had been using previously for this problem; but this time I stared at the smoke and decided if I became the smoke, there would be nothing for the creature to hold onto, and it would have to leave. I meditated much like I do with Nature when I become one with the object of my focus, and as I sat there I became the smoke floating in the air and rising in the room. As I did this, the pain subsided for a moment and then suddenly simply disappeared very quickly. I had healed myself of this dark creature. I felt it came because I had used my gift with intention to hurt those two people instead of using my gift for helping people with universal love. My hurtful intention had attracted the dark energy.

CHAPTER FIFTEEN

Halawa Bay, Molokai

IN THE 1990S MY HUSBAND AND I traveled to Hawaii. I was so grateful because he was interested in purchasing some property there. I had that in my mind since the first time I had stepped foot on its soil.

We found condos on Molokai at an affordable price. We purchased a rundown unit but I didn't care. I was ecstatic. I could also feel my father with me. He would have loved it for its view of the ocean and the trade winds caressing the body, and oh, the flowers.... how he loved flowers!

When we returned the following year I would just sit and stare at the view, looking at the ocean and paradise foliage saying over and over again "I can't believe I have a place on Molokai". We went in town a couple of times and out to the East end of the Island and were even more awe struck by the beauty of Hawaii and in particular, Molokai, for there were no people on the beaches. The turquoise ocean lapping against the black lava rock was etched in my mind forever.

Turquoise Ocean

We decided to see about snorkeling and I called the Snorkeling & Scuba with Bill Kapuni phone number. We were told he was the best guide in town; and soon, we climbed on board with another couple and went out to sea with Bill Kapuni at the wheel.

To say the least, he was a very unusual man to look at. He was very tall, six feet four inches, and dark skinned with a beautiful face. His eyes laughed and twinkled a little. His smile filled his face with the largest teeth I had ever seen. His hair was shoulder length, grey and black, with a mustache of reddish black and beard of graying white. His body was enormous -- 340 pounds! His hairless chest was bare while the lower half of him wore a black rubber diving suit. His feet were huge (16EEEE), and he was barefoot. His arms were as if he were a body builder, but not disproportionate to the rest of his body. His left arm had a very unusual tattoo around the muscle, and his left leg had an equally interesting tattoo running down the side of it. I had never met nor cared to meet anyone with tattoos on their body knowing a sociological study stating the statistical probabilities that those persons had been in prison. I did not know of tattoos and their cultural significance in the Pacific Islands at that time. He appeared like someone who had stepped out of a movie. He was the most beautiful and unusual man I had ever seen.

He was the attraction for the tour! He was personable and knew the ocean in a way that seemed as natural as breathing. He spoke about the reef with knowledge and conviction. I was later to learn he took the NOAA crews around the reef to monitor and chart and form base line study data for the Molokai reef. He knew a lot, but was never braggadocios about it. That is what struck everyone, he was so strong in "mana" (spirit), yet so humble in his manner of speaking. When he spoke he commanded immediate attention. His voice was loud because it came from such a large chest cavity. It was not forced or accelerated or pushed or escalated…it was just voluminously loud and carried with it the voice of authority and respect.

His diving and swimming was even more impressive than his person. He swam like he was a fish! One of his amakua (Spirit guide/ protector) was the shark. With ease and swiftness but with limited motion, he glided through the ocean. He swam with a spear gun he had made. The gun shoots spears at the fish and it was inlaid with cut bones and mother of pearl cut from shells in Hawaiian shark tooth designs. (This gun can be seen in the Native American Museum at the Smithsonian Institution in Washington). He disappeared from the group of snorkelers and came back to the boat with his spear filled with yellow reef fish. Fish I later learned he liked to eat best of all. As I sat on the boat and turned my attention from him and the ocean to the fish he had speared, I noticed some were still moving. That upset me because I thought they were suffering with the spear through their bodies and still alive. I mentioned this to him and was surprised that he didn't much care.

He mentioned to us all that he was a carver and had his works for sale at his house and then proceeded to tell us where he lived. The A frame across from Molokai Shores. Years later, when I told him about this trip he was surprised that he had not asked us over for dinner. He usually did that with tourists to see if they would buy one of his pieces. He must have known we didn't have much extra to spend. We ended the trip with a picture being taken of the four of us, me and my husband, him and his son in law. I sent him a duplicate of the picture. He told me he kept it. He did.

The 4 of us after scuba dive

Every year we traveled to Molokai for a vacation of two to three weeks and sometimes two times a year. We scheduled another snorkel trip with Bill Kapuni Tours. My husband had been a competitive swimmer in college and was impressed with Bill's swimming capabilities. They swam together quite a bit. I ended up on the boat earlier then everyone else, and he came up to get me to come in the water and said, "Watch this guy swim you have to see it." It was like watching a dolphin or shark swim. He moved just like those animals under water. It was truly a sight to behold. I guess what made it so special was the ease with which he moved in the water…very little motion. Just like a fish. Their movement is very little, yet they propel so far.

Very soon Bill Kapuni came in the boat by himself! He sat down and began talking to me….about his wife who had recently passed over. I was not terribly surprised by this sudden personal conversation, because it had been that way all through my life that way, people would suddenly start talking about something they needed to share. My impression of him was that he was stronger than strong and could handle anything by himself. He possessed so much power in his spirit and presence, that I did not think he needed anyone.

I felt some pain from him, but not a tremendous pain…simply a loss he would get over. We were drawn into each other's energy while he shared his intense conversation. No one else in the entire world existed. Time all around us stood still and frozen as we sat in the boat while he told me this story. The rest of the group returned to the boat and he stopped talking. He started the engines and we departed the area, and I thought about what he had said to me all the way back to the harbor in silence. I only remember the wind in my hair. Perhaps I had taken in more of his pain then I thought. I realized I had helped him some by listening. I said goodbye in silence. He never did remember sharing to me.

Upon our next return to Molokai we attended the earth day festivities. I was an environmentalist and very interested in Molokai's dedication to the earth and nature. Bill Kapuni had a booth at that celebration. He had the scale model of a double hulled canoe he had made there on a table; and he was serving awa from a koa bowl he had made and offered it to anyone who would want some. But I noticed some Hawaiians hanging around the table were surprised when he offered some to me. He gave them a nod that it was OK. So maybe he didn't offer it to everyone. My husband wandered off and would not have tried the awa anyway, but I sat down across from Bill at the table. He had not remembered me from the year before, but gave me some awa served in a carved coconut cup. I drank the brown, dirt, tasting drink. It was pleasant enough. I thanked him and got up and left.

Bill Kapuni…was almost pure full blooded Hawaiian of royal ancestry. King Kamehameha was purported to be over seven feet; but because there has been so much intermarrying amongst races in Hawaii, Hawaiians are much shorter today and carry a smaller percentage of Hawaiian koko (blood).

If you see someone large today, they are most likely of Samoan ancestry.

My husband called Bill Kapuni a "mountain of a man" and described him that way to our friends. This is how most people saw and knew this beautiful looking man so tall and handsome with a large heart and spiritual presence about him. When he spoke, people listened. I didn't realize at the time that someday I would too.

Back Side of Molokai with 2000 foot Cliffs

CHAPTER SIXTEEN

I NEVER THOUGHT I WOULD REACH this particular "big birthday." My lifeline from birth did not show I would live long, and I expected to follow in my father's footsteps…exiting at an early age. So when the birthday was clearly going to arrive for me I decided to treat myself to a special trip with a friend. My husband didn't like to travel but a friend of mine recently lost her husband and needed a change in scenery. I chose Chili as our destination because I had received a Christmas card many years back with a photograph of a beautiful mountain in Chili. This is where I decided we should go. We would sail around the Cape Horn at the bottom of South America. The US had built the Panama Canal so ships wouldn't keep getting wrecked in storms as they rounded that infamous point. I had heard that it was a rough trip with high waves, but I wanted to see that mountain. Besides, I had survived the Colorado River.

I met my good friend at a show when she purchased spirit vessels from me. We connected on a spiritual level and had a great time together laughing through our fears as the airplane ride down to Buenos Aires got very rough over the equator. Buenos Aires is the home of the very sexy dance, the Tango, and Maria Eva Duarte de Peron, made famous by the movie Evita starring Madonna.

While on a tour in an old bus in the middle of nowhere, there was a couple behind us; and the woman started coughing and having an asthma attack. My friend was asthmatic and told me it was getting serious now given the frequency and depth of her trying to get air into her lungs. Her husband was asking people on the bus for medication. No one had any. Surprisingly enough even my friend did not have hers with her.

I said, "We have to help." My friend knew I could heal so she showed me a place on the woman's body to touch to heal the asthma. I asked the husband to move and sat in his seat so I could touch her. I sent light into her body until her choking subsided and she was able to catch her breath. She finally calmed down and was able to breath normally. Needless to say, the husband couldn't stop thanking me and people had puzzled looks on their faces. If they looked like they were going to ask me something, I simply looked down. I didn't need to draw attention to myself and talk about it to a few curious strangers. I had been able to be a conduit for God's light, and the woman and her husband knew what had been done with intention to heal in Light. That was all that mattered.

Our cabin was on the 9th deck with a huge window suite on a beautiful ship called the Wind near the bow of the ship. There was a table and couch in the room and on the table there was a large plate of fresh fruit. There were beautiful dining rooms, on board entertainment and activities. We chose shore excursions at every port. It was a trip of a lifetime.

We took a shore excursion to The Faulklands, which is a small fishing and boat repair town near the southern tip of the continent. There were shipwrecks in the harbor that were rusted. The port had gentle hills reaching out from it and covered with a symphony of multi-colored houses. While I was waiting for the tender to take us out to the ship from the Island, a wave of visions about my son and his child to be came flooding in on me. I wondered what was going on. The baby wasn't due for another three weeks.

I had become close to the baby while in the womb, for my son allowed me to touch his wife's belly at four months. As soon as I touched her, in my vision, I saw a giant field of white in a cotton-like texture came out from my right hand and encircled him in the uterus enveloping him. I was so surprised, I pulled away quickly. It happened in a split second. I did not know what had happened. In looking back, I believe it was a shield of white light that was thrown around the baby to protect him from his mother.

The next time I saw them at a restaurant in Green Valley, I asked if I could place my hand on her belly and when I did, I felt the heart beat of my grandson. I could not believe I felt that either. It was a surprise to me, and I thought they had heard the heart beat, but they said no, they couldn't hear or feel his heart beat. Upon returning to the ship there was a phone message from my husband, and sure enough my grandson had been born. I braved the computer center on board and e-mailed "a welcome to this world" message to my Grandson from his Grama.

That night we entered the Chilian Fiords and I was tossed out of bed. We were suddenly in a mighty storm. We turned on the lights, and I asked, "Why are they washing the windows at this hour"? I went to the large window and had trouble standing because of the rocking of the ship. The oranges and apples from the fruit plate were rolling around on the floor. I knew from my rafting days the behavior of a boat in troubled water, and knew we were in trouble. The ship was over 750 feet long, the waves were spaced apart sufficiently that in the hole between the waves, the bow and the stern would each be on a wave as the ship went over the expanse between the two waves below it. I could feel the ship in the middle out of the water and the wind going underneath as the ship shimmied.

All we knew to do was to put white light around the ship as well as the ships control room where I felt the stress of the men there. We went through about two or three waves and were almost tipped over. We were running the waves perpendicular instead of at an angle where the ship could roll over the waves. When the ship went 15 to 20 degrees off perpendicular, we cut the top of the wave off, did not climb as high, and rolled over it instead of crashing down in between the waves. I relaxed a little.

The water going across the window was the 65 foot waves crashing over the bow of the ship and whipping back along the sides. I sat at the window, because it was too difficult to stand steady, and watched the waves. I kept saying how angry the waves were. We later learned that the wind gage didn't register on their measurement device. It was too much wind velocity to register, for they could only register 100 MPH. They guess that the wind was 125 to 150 MPH.

As I sat on the floor rocking with the motion of the ship, I realized how close we were to perishing at sea. I looked at the storm and marveled at its' might and said, "we are all meant to die sometime, if this is the time Lord so be it. Thank you for my life."

I had analyzed the ways of escape should we go over and there would be no way we could escape no matter which side we went over on. I then placed that out of my mind and focused on the white light surrounding the ship. Outside, the ocean was black. There were hardly any whitecaps to it. The lights were on outside the ship and one was close enough to us giving light to the ocean below. As I watched the ship and the ocean dance, we would go up to the top and down quickly just like being on a very fast elevator.

Our Chilian captain on board said that this was the worst storm he had seen or heard of in 60 years. All ships and aircraft were sent away from the storm which meant if we did go over, no one would be able to rescue us and all would perish in such huge waves and winds.

Just like in my other life threatening experiences, I relaxed with no panic and simply accepted. I suppose that is how my death will be also…calmness and gratitude for the Journey. Life on earth is the single flash of a firefly's light in the summer's night, or one misty white breath of a deer in winter's day break.

We missed a port because we were only able to travel 19 miles in that 24 hour period. We had been locked inside the ship during the storm at both night and day. They were probably afraid we would be swept off the decks if we went outside which would most likely be true. We were told to stay in our rooms and not move about the ship.

All facilities on the ship were closed the next day including all the restaurants as the kitchens were closed because a few cooks were burned while trying to cook in the kitchen. One of the cabins on the lower deck flooded. A man had a heart attack and was evacuated when the storm subsided. All the crew had to get sea sickness shots so they could start up with their work again. When the storm subsided and the waves were only 30 feet, we were all relieved and thankful we made it through a very dark storm. What I didn't know was that I was about to face one even more threatening.

I returned home and traveled to Tucson to see my first and only grandchild. What joy to hold him. I could feel the cellular connection. This was just pure love and joy in Spirit. I introduced him to the sunrise and colors of the sunsets. When I went outside with him, black ravens flew over us. Ben was the joy in my life I had been waiting for. We became very attached. I didn't think about it at the time, but he refused to suckle his mother but always tried me. I could see he was extremely bright. His mother was MENSA and my son certainly had inherited his parents high IQ. I saw him frequently and he became the most important being in my world until he was about 18 months.

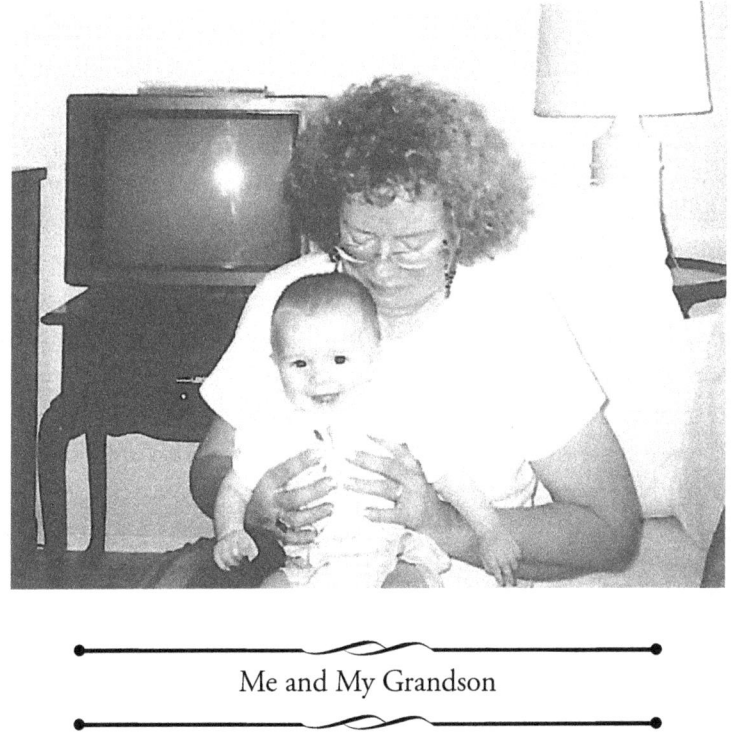

Me and My Grandson

I knew something was wrong with my son's wife but I didn't know what. We often see what we want to see and what was there was certainly not something I wanted to acknowledge in my reality. I observed her doing very bizarre things to my grandson. I saw her hurt him. I have difficulty understanding how someone could treat a person, let alone an innocent child, let alone a baby in such a cruel way. I had gotten away to Molokai where I always felt close to Spirit and decided that I could not watch it any more without doing something about it and standing up for an innocent child. I would not bury my head in the sand and allow a child to be treated in such ways before my eyes, . . . Much less my grandson.

It would have been easier to report what I saw of a child I did not know to CPS rather then my own grandson. I knew there would be family repercussions with my son's mother-in-law and anger from her and her family. However, I did not expect my son's response. I made my choice on Molokai, and I believed that it was worth saving my grandson from terror or worse in his innocent life. I had always been a champion of the downtrodden and poor and weak at my law practice and it was my personality to help and protect innocents.

Although none of the physical allegations I made could be proved by the time CPS visited the home, there was probably sufficient evidence to show that my grandson was 'not thriving' (the legal term I believe for child protective services to enter the family and oversee a childs' care.) He had not gained one single ounce from the time he was twelve months old until I reported it at 18months! A policeman specifically told me to report this situation. This was the hardest thing I had ever done in my life so far.

I may have saved my grandson's life but I lost my son in the process. There was family history there to support my observation. I have not been able to see my grandson since he was 18 months old. At that time, this was my greatest heartbreak.

I didn't think I would ever feel anything worse. This was extremely painful – the loss of another person I so dearly loved. I had been at the greatest high of love, but I was dashed to the depths of despair over losing not only my son, but my grandson, the light of my life. I had evolved spiritually, for this tragedy this time in my life, and did not turn to hate and anger. Although the loss was unbearable I did not turn to anger at God or hatred of the people involved. I avoided that pit fall which simply eats you up and wastes your time in darkness. That precious child meant everything to me and he was gone. It was the worst season of my life.

There are no grandparent's rights in Arizona. I couldn't even fight my way back into his life. There was nothing I could do. I was helpless. All I could do was pray. I would have to leave it to God and child protective services to protect my grandson. I had done all I could. He would have to be on his own spiritual path alone…as we all are ultimately.

I could feel and see visions when he was being hurt, and I cried until whoever was hurting him stopped. I also learned that if I yelled 'stop', it stopped quicker. This phenomenon is well documented from mothers of boys at war becoming injured or killed. The mother knows of the injury or death before being informed by the government.

The last time my grandson was at my house, I bought pretty butterflies that would stick on the walls and I placed them around the house at his height. He found them and I gave him all but a few, one of which I kept in my closet. If is falls down, I know there is a problem going on. When I felt him being hurt, I don't cry anymore; but I pray and hold him in light. You can not change anyone else in the world. You can only change yourself. This was my major lesson in control during my life.

As you have seen with my life, it is a roller coaster or a ship in the storm. But through it all, I have learned when one door closes another door opens; and that closing of the one door is meant to happen to push you onto your path probably in a different direction you could never have imagined. I had to learn from the kaleidoscope of events, situations and people in my life in order to grow, and I am most grateful for the learning experience of it all.

Molokai Overlooking Kalaupapa

CHAPTER SEVENTEEN

IN SANTA FE NEW MEXICO WHILE we were both at a very nice restaurant for our Birthdays, I met, Puna. We became immediately connected with each other on a spiritual level. Puna had traveled to Santa Fe from Kauai, Hawaii with the Japanese photographer from the movie "What the Bleep Do We Know".

The photographer had photographed water molecules that had changed their molecular structures depending upon what words were said over them. As we leisurely drove up to Santa Fe from Albuquerque where we lived, through the back mountain roads of New Mexico, passing scenery of winding pinion tree covered hills, we heard on the radio that this photographer was going to give a free lecture in Santa Fe that day.

As we sat eating I looked up and saw this Hawaiian woman walk through the door. Our eyes met in a recognition of some sort. She was wearing a lei of kukui nuts. I did not know at the time that this signifies in Hawaiian culture...a kumu or revered teacher. They are the only ones to wear a—kukui nut lei.

I asked my husband to go talk to her and see who she was. There was some discussion about whether she was Hawaiian or not. I was the only one who thought she was. My husband got up and went over to her table and eventually brought her back with the Japanese photographer.

We met and had a friendly chat enough to find out that she was born on Molokai and lived in Kauai. She found out that we lived in Albuquerque and had a condo on Molokai. That was about it. Even with the knowledge of the break through this famous photographer had made, I was far more interested in Puna.

My husband and I continued our lives in Albuquerque New Mexico as usual, however, all of a sudden six months later, I began talking about this Hawaiian woman I had met, and that I thought I was going to move to Hawaii and work for her. This just 'came out of the blue like things sometimes do for me. I don't exactly know where they come from or why. It felt like a certainty. My friends were very surprised. Women like us, well established in our communities and organizations just didn't 'pull up stakes' at our ages and move!

I was still tied down with my mother whom I was caring for. I had taken her to Molokai for two weeks the year before. She loved it and didn't want to leave. She fell there rounding a corner because she was going too fast for her capabilities. That was the first fall I knew of. In November she fell again, and this time, broke her hip, but more importantly now had dementia.

I had to place her in a small residence of 6 elderly persons being cared for because her doctor said that was the best type of facility— less confusing for her. She had been living very nearby me in her own condo when she fell, I had been fixing her meals and checking in on her three times a day. I had purchased a life line for her to wear, the type that you press a button and someone comes to you, but she didn't wear it because she thought it meant I was "checking up on her whereabouts".

In April, my mother died in my arms with the hospice nurse in attendance. I was very glad I could be with her upon her passing. Since her husband (my father) was gone already, I couldn't think of any better way for her to die then me holding her. Prior to her dying, I told her she was a good mother. As soon as I said that, she slumped in her wheelchair and passed. I know she did the best she could, at least, and I knew it would make her feel better to tell her. She made me humble, which I much prefer to being arrogant. I learned many lessons from her, and I am grateful.

My husband couldn't stay in one place for very long and now was going to move to Colorado to start a business. I was left to close up the Albuquerque house, while having garage sales, packing, unpacking, loading the U-Haul, driving the U-Haul rental trucks to take belongings up there, and setting up an apartment living situation for him. I think I did all that for him to alleviate some of my guilt for the fact that I had made up my mind to leave him.

We bought a building where he was going to open a Chocolate Shoppe and expand it later. He would rent out the other side and live in the apartment upstairs above the businesses.

With my mother dead I had to sell her house, sell and dispose of her household belongings, and take her ashes back to Philadelphia. In addition, I was packing up the house for the apartment and then for me….my things. I had decided I was not going to move again. I liked New Mexico and I liked Hawaii better yet. I made the decision that I had to continue my path and my growth without my husband. I would go to Hawaii to heal.

I felt badly about leaving my third husband because he did not really do anything wrong. We were friends with no passion, and he never understood my need to plant roots. He simply was not growing on a spiritual path like I had done and worse, he didn't want to. We had grown apart in our interests and what I had mistakenly perceived as his spirituality was really only his understanding of the Indian culture. He understood it but did not believe it in his heart. He did not believe in God.

It was the right decision even if it meant another trauma in my life. Before leaving for Hawaii, I was glad I had looked over the lives I had left behind one more time. I knew I had made the right choices all along the path of my life. I did not know why I ended up with certain spouses, in certain places with certain jobs, but it was all good because it brought me to this point in time in my life.

I had absolutely no control over anything in my life and I had to review that lessen again. I cried everyday and read the Bible, watched the ocean and gazed at the foliage around me. I was desperately trying to heal. I had to learn that as you reach new spiritual levels in your higher self, crown chakra or some would say higher level of awareness, old friends and others drop away and new people at your same spiritual level take their place. With the connection with persons at higher spiritual levels, there is no loneliness, because you finally feel connected and grounded and you are with and in Spirit having a connection to God and with others connected to God in like manner. I suppose we grow to a point where we can simply, 'be', alone with and in God.

We need to constantly strive to grow and change as we water with learning experiences that spiritual seed inside each of us. This is the seed inside us that needs to struggle and reach upwards towards God to grow. I did not know how long or what I was going to do except go to Molokai for a while with a one way ticket. This is something I had always wanted to do. I was very fragile, unfocused, and ungrounded.

I ended up walking the beaches on the east end of Molokai or at my condo almost every single day for two and one half months. I felt that if I walked putting one foot in front of the other, I would eventually start moving forward, because I was teaching my body how – maybe my mind and heart would follow.

Sometimes I would walk in the ocean itself. I thought if I could at least do that, I would be going forward with my shattered life. I looked at the ocean, made daily trips to Sandy Beach at the East end of the Island and made a point of getting into the ocean everyday. I later learned that Puna taught her halau that cleansing in the ocean everyday was essential. I instinctively knew that. My main focus was to overcome the fear of the ocean and the fear of being out of control.

Almost everyday, I went to Sandy Beach or Halawa where I would turn around as I heard my name called out in Makani(wind) near the bushes. I would get in the water and float on my back with arms outstretched and float in the waves and go wherever they would take me without watching and not attempting to stop Kanaloa (the ocean god) in anyway. It took a while, but it was beginning to work… learning to accept my life and my floating without control of anything. I was learning to let go and learning to follow where ever I was directed to go. I had been doing this all of my life, but now I was aware of it…reading my signs and letting go.

Sandy Beach

After two weeks of renting a car on Island, at an outrageous cost, I decided to go to Oahu and purchase a cheap vehicle. I found a used car and had it shipped over on the barge back to Molokai. While there I spoke with a fortune teller at a marketplace. It was unusual for me to seek guidance in this way. She said "I would find the man I was searching for in August. He would heal me. I probably already knew him, and he already did know me and was watching me". She thought he was from the Pacific Northwest. I didn't know I was searching for a man. With this information, I sifted through all the men I knew from the Pacific North West and came up blank! I tossed the fortune telling off to the wind and didn't think about it anymore but knew August was only a couple of months away.

CHAPTER EIGHTEEN

I PULLED MYSELF TOGETHER BY THE end of July and decided to go to Kauai and look for the Hawaiian woman I had met my preceding birthday in Santa Fe. Kauai has over 60,000 people, but I was sure I could find her.

Although Kauai was not my favorite Island back in the 80's when I was visiting them all, Maui O' ke Noi, (Maui is the best) but looking back it was probably my relatively immature age and my spiritual development at that time, which made me like Maui best. Also, twenty-five years ago, there was far less development on Maui. Now, I was perfectly attuned to the spirituality I felt in Kauai. The spirits were light....not intense as on Molokai. They were more similar to the lightness in New Mexico yet different still. My heart began to open some in this Island, and I opened my eyes once again and began to see the beauty of the Hawaiian Islands.

Kauai is the oldest Island and is believed to be where all Hawaiians come to this earth and all Hawaiians leave from this earth. The two places are on opposite sides of the Island and since both are areas that are close to the veil between this world and the preceding one and the next, the light shines brightly there. It was this light I felt and basked in. It was healing for me, and I loved it.

I decided to search for Puna, the Hawaiian lady who I felt brought me to the Islands. I decided to follow my path that would be shown to me like any vision quest. I started in Ka pa'a, a town in Kauai. I went into grocery stores, restaurants, shops asking about this Hawaiian lady. I did have a picture of her that I had someone take of us in Santa Fe. That would help I thought. Finally, after a few hours, someone thought she lived in Koloa in the South. I was directed to a house, invited in to talk story, but it wasn't the right woman. I turned around and still felt the right direction was on the east side of the Island.

The next morning I went back to Ka pa'a. I walked the streets with the photograph and saw a small building with a police car outside and another one turning in. I thought it might be a police station and perhaps, since they are trained observers, they might recognize the lady in the picture. I came just after a very tall and large Hawaiian policeman from the second car had entered the building and knocked on the door. He came out and I asked the question. He wanted to know why I wanted to find her. I told him the coincidences in meeting her and my intuitive feelings of finding her. Surprisingly enough, he didn't question my story. He directed me and even drew me a map to someone who might know her.

I found the location and this time when I showed the picture they thought they knew her and said she wasn't far away! They directed me to the building she would be in. I knocked on the door, was told to enter and saw her! I placed my hand over my heart while holding the screen door with the other and asked "Do you even remember me?" She responded, "Yes, yes, of course, you are the reason I am here today." "Come, come," and she beckoned me towards her!

Upon walking into the dimly lit room, because there was only one row of windows on the shady side of the building; I found three ladies eating a fresh looking green salad and talking. All stood to greet me, but Puna put her arm around me and said, "you are the reason I'm not on my way to the mainland right now". She explained that she was to fly to give a house blessing in Vermont and was waiting to be called to board having received her boarding pass, when she said all these images of her visit to Santa Fe flooded in on her, and she decided not to go.

Puna is connected to Spirit and knows things through visions like all Kahunas. She knew something surrounding her Santa Fe trip was to happen and she needed to stay on Kauai. We talked some and set up a time to see each other at sun rise the next morning as she did a hula every sunrise at this particular sacred place.

At sunrise I witnessed a hula for the glory of the sun rise and Ke Akua (God). Although I had seen lots of hulas performed in Hawaii, I had never seen such beauty of motion before. It was like the extraordinary beauty I saw when I watched Bill Kapuni swim. I assume it was because Puna's dance was channeled through Spirit.

We went back to the car and talked. Puna set up the day for me to meet certain of her people. The first was her assistant who had waited in the car. Later, Puna told me some things about myself I was unaware of. She could see differently then others and saw around me many spirits, who had helped me in the past and who would continue to help me. She described a few, and I recognized them. Puna left in her car, and her assistant led the way up the mountain to her house. She was also a spiritual lady who had been Puna's assistant for some time. She had a beautiful home looking at the waterfalls of the pali. She said at certain times, she could count 11 of them. Her yard was filled with fruit trees.

She was a seamstress. She sewed the dresses for the halau among other things. Material was around, but we sat down at a table and she worked with me in a way I had never experienced. She worked with colors and afterwards, I found, I had lost a good deal of the pain I had been carrying. I was considerably lighter and felt uplifted.

That night I noticed a Hawaiian 'event' of dancing, fires and chants near the place Puna had danced that morning. I was too timid to go and watch. I just listened to the drums pounding and the chants wafting to me through the evening breezes.

The next day I returned to Molokai, and I was still in Spirit. I continued walking the beaches. Suddenly, I made arrangements in August to go to Kauai again and called Puna on Sunday morning to tell her I was coming that day, and I told her I thought I was going to work for her in some capacity. She said to call her when I arrived.

She gave me three hours of her time to teach me all the things that she was in charge of for Hawaiians and what she did for the projects. She agreed she needed help. Her brother told her she needed my help. It was settled I would move to Kauai and work for her under some grant in some capacity not yet determined.

I returned to Molokai to make plans for the move to Kauai. I was leaving Molokai for Kauai. As I sat in my condo gazing out the sliding glass door at the ocean and Hawaiian scenery, I felt sad I would be leaving Molokai without really understanding the Island very much or understanding the spirituality of it. It was a very different spirituality than Kauai, and I didn't understand the energies I felt here.

I decided to call Puna to try and get some understanding of the pushes and pulls and different levels of energy I felt on Molokai. She did a good job of explaining it; however, when I hung up I realized I didn't know much about the Hawaiian places on the Island and their spiritual significance. I tried to call Puna back and couldn't get her so I called her assistant and she said "Call Bill Kapuni. He knows the spirituality of the Island better than anyone."

PART II

CHAPTER NINETEEN

Bill the Wood Carver

Tᴴᴱ ʜᴏʟʟᴀɴᴅ ᴀᴍᴇʀɪᴄᴀ ᴄʀᴜɪsᴇ sʜɪᴘs ʟᴏᴏᴋᴇᴅ to place Molokai as one of their ports 'o call, because Molokai is the least developed Island in the chain, retains the traditional Hawaiian culture and lifestyle and is known as the last Hawaiian Island. Molokai is the center, not only of the Hawaiian Islands, but is also known as the Island of Pule (prayer), because most Hawaiian Kahuns inhabited this Island historically. Although the Kahuna ways, (those of the Spiritual medicine men/women) were done in secret, they were never lost. Bill Kapunis' wahine tutu (Grandmother) taught him Hawaiian traditional culture, how to read clouds, harness Nature's energies, use lau la palau (healing plants) and other Hawaiian ways of healing.

In honoring his ancestors, he honored Nature and all that it is. It was always important to him to protect the aina, its waters, Kanaloa, Wai, Waihele (ocean, river, waterfall), because they were all his icebox and he fed his family from them. He hunted wild boar and deer with bow and arrow and gun and foraged in its mountains for food, and lau la palau plants. He learned the sacred ways of carving and was known throughout the Island as the Kalai Pahu - the master Pahu (Drum) maker, a position of great respect. The Pahu speaks for Hawaiians. It is the voice Hawaiians pass on in energy.

3 healing stones at the beach at waikiki

William Kuamo'o Helelani Kealoha Kapuni was not only descended from royalty, but was a direct descendent of a 16th century Kahuna on O'ahu. Her Mana resides in one of the Kahuna (Wizard)

Stones on Kuhio Beach in Waikaiki, O'ahu today where Hawaiians and tourists as well visit to ask for and receive healing.

The healing stones at Waikiki Beach are honored and prayed to because three healers left their spirits in the rocks to enable them to continue healing once they left this world. One was named Bill's Tutu named Kapuni. This is where Hawaiians as well as tourists visit to place their leis for them at the fence.

The Cruise ship did not expect any protest from the 7,300 Island residents, 55% of whom are of Hawaiian koko (blood). After all, this economic development would not include building hotels and condos like on the neighboring Islands of Maui and Oahu.

Molokai people are proud and independent. Their ancestors are from the aina, and they malama (take are of) and aloha (love) their pristine and unspoiled Island. "Let Molokai change you, don't try and change Molokai" one bumper sticker says.

According to state regulations, if a cruise ship wanted to come to the Island, all it needed was for its ship's agent to obtain a dock reservation from the Departments of Transportation and of Land and Natural Resources. There didn't need to be any review or environmental impact statement. Molokai people do not make decisions that affect the community without "talking story," where they discuss the matter together until things get "pono," (come to a consensus with understanding). When the community met to "talk story," one member in favor of the Cruise ships made a mistake by saying "The ship is coming. Get used to it."

Bill Kapuni and others, said, a simple "no." There would be damage to the reef from such a large ship dropping anchor unless they followed the advice of the locals like Bill to stay further out into the ocean… "about a mile", he would say.

For Bill it was a sacred duty to protect Molokai and her reefs. He, along with others, filed for injunctive relief in the courts. The only way to protect Molokai's traditional lifestyle and traditional cultural practices for the future was to protect her reef. Other's looked to him for his strength and devotion to maintaining Hawaiian Culture. What many people didn't know was that he was trained since childhood in the ways of the Kahuna.

The cruise ships with their dock reservations were going to come before anyone could stop them. Bill and other local activists created a peaceful protest with placards and T-shirts saying "No Cruise ships on Molokai Island". People were preparing for the ship to dock with welcoming hula and music planned and vendors set up to sell their food and wares. The mixed feelings of the residents in the end didn't matter, because Kanaloa (god of the sea) and Makani (god of wind) heard Bill's prayers and call.

There were 150 protesters along the dock and in canoes praying, as the Statendam, lowered first one and then another tender into the ocean with eager tourists on board. While Bill and others formed a circle and chanted, Bill quietly raised his arms to his ancestors and the gods. The winds came down with fury from the mountains creating whitecaps in the channel, where moments earlier it had been calm seas. Because the whitecaps and waves made it unsafe for the passengers, the Stateman called back the tenders, loaded them on the ship, pulled up anchor, and sailed away. When the Statendam was past Molokai, the winds ceased, white caps vanished, the ocean, once again, became calm.

Bill playing the drum

—〰—

I remembered Bill Kapuni, the boat captain and beautiful swimmer. I thought about it for a few days. It was getting down to less than a week now before I left for Kauai and I was feeling pushed to learn more about the spirituality of Molokai before I could leave.

I called Bill and he said he knew of Puna. I explained how we met and what I wanted to learn from the Island. I now know that this was the equivalent of an introduction to gain entrance like in my own "society." Genealogy is important to Hawaiians also. It is their place in the world. On Molokai many introduced themselves at public events and meetings by reciting their ancestry. He amazingly agreed to show me around the spiritual places on the Island. I was surprised and happy that I would learn more about Molokai before I left. I even felt some relief that I would have some spiritual understanding of this Island that had been my sanctuary, and that I would be leaving soon. I said when and where shall we meet? He said "tonight about 5 at your condo, what is your number"?

CHAPTER TWENTY

Promptly at five o'clock there was a knock on the door. I answered it and there he stood with his blue and white bandana on his head wearing black shorts and black tank top. He looked down and flashed a smile at me as he took his slippers off at the doorstep.

Bill with his blue and white bandana

He was carrying a brown paper bag under his arm and I showed him in. Bill asked where we could have a table and sit down; I showed him the lanai (porch). He opened his bag and said we would be having a Hawaiian Awa Ceremony as he took out a Koa bowl with brown liquid in it and a cup made from a small coconut … the same bowl and cup he had used at the earth day festival a couple years before.

Bill and I sat on the lanai and drank awa together and talked while a Hawaiian from down stairs B building watched us. When you drink awa in a Hawaiian ceremony, you speak from your heart. We spoke from our hearts for how long I do not know. We were in spirit together. I do not remember what we spoke about except I remember he asked me a lot of questions. I had a feeling of being on a witness stand at a trial, because he was probing my spiritual life which was very personal to me then.

When we were finished talking, he asked me to heal him. We moved inside, he sat on a chair, and I began to pray and give him light as I had done many times to others. This time there were two new elements to the healing. He was actually out of his body by about four inches (on a slant not vertical) and his deceased tutu wahine worked with me giving me direction.

When I finished working on Bill, he felt much better and thanked me. He said he had somewhere to take me and that I should follow him in my car. I did. He took me to what can only be described as a Vertex of energy on his land in Kalamaula Mauka Molokai. As a 95% Hawaiian he had qualified for Hawaiian homestead land, that had been granted to Hawaiians with at least 50% native koko, from the original Crown lands in Federal Legislation. He had been co-creator of a pyramid sculpture constructed there on his land. We sat near by it in lawn chairs on the hill side for a long time looking at the stars while he told me about the "Soul of the World" Vertex, its significance and how it was built.

As we walked down the mountain side path and then dirt road to our cars, Bill picked a branch from a purple crown flower tree and gave it to me. He explained how unusual it was for the tree to be growing on an otherwise barren land with no water. It was both the Queen's and his favorite flower.

I arrived home high in spirit at about nine or ten and got a glass, filled it with water to place the crown flower in, went into my bedroom and placed it on my night stand. Bill's energy was still strongly around me, and before I went to sleep, he called and said he would be by about ten in the morning and take me to another place.

He was punctual, honked outside and then walked up the stairs to my condo. I discovered this was the traditional Hawaiian way of approaching and visiting someone at their home. I had been trained as a girl to always be late I guess it is a matter of determining who is more important to keep the other waiting. I was to always keep every date waiting down stairs until they talked to my father even if I was ready! But when he called my name in his deep commanding voice, I immediately got up to greet him at the door.

We traveled to the East end of the Island. There is a place in the road traveling east where I always become quiet and calm inside. I didn't know why. I was about to find out.

As we left my condo complex and turned east on the main road, energy filled the car with our spiritual connection we had made the day before. We were silent in our energy and simply enjoying Molokai scenery. We passed mile 20 with the wide expanse of white sandy beach and continued on our way to rocky point where the ocean both laps and pounds up against the jagged black lava rock shore lines with beaches interspersed sporadically and infrequently.

We proceeded to the mountain towards the large ranch area were green pasture lands met trees and some rocks are sprinkled artistically along the mountainside. Soon we came to the tall grass along the road side where I always became quiet. Bill pointed to a high place on the cliff where kukui (light) trees grew in a grove called Loni Kaula. I had not heard that name before. Loni Kaula had been a famous kahuna on Molokai, and he worked in light and healed people. Bill stopped and obtained permission to enter this place. Hawaiian protocol is always to obtain permission to enter another's land before doing so.

I noticed Bill was observing me. Yesterday I passed the healing test and connection with his grandmother. Today I was further questioned about what I felt, saw, learned etc. from the Kukui nut grove. He was probing my spiritual awareness and abilities.

The place is a place of incredible healing power. All pain floats away from your body and mind immediately. You float in Spirit. Your mind is empty. It is a place of complete and utter peace. Your chest swells as your heart opens to the universe. My breath became stronger and deeper and slower and quieter…all at the same time. It is as though someone had lifted me and was holding me on a cloud. I was in a spiritual connection with God.

I have no idea how long we were there. There was no time. We didn't eat. We weren't hungry. We "came down" from this spiritual high by going to Halawa Valley where waterfalls plunge into pools at the back of the Valley several hundred feet emptying into pools and then streams that rush to the ocean.

We drove back towards town in silence. As we approached my condo, I thought he would turn and the day would be over. It was late afternoon by now. Instead, he said I have a place on the West end I'd like to show you now. I said all right and off we went. Food didn't enter our minds so we never stopped in town for a bite. You aren't hungry when you are in spirit. Bill drove in silence. He was not the tour guide today, for he did not verbally share as he ushered me around his Island. Instead, the information I was gathering from him was in the spiritual realm. We were both very quiet and in Spirit and in each other's energy.

It was a setting sun in the West by the time we reached our destination at the shoreline…a beach. Quiet and surrounded by bushes, Bill sat on a low discarded white lounge chair partially missing its strapping. He reached out his hand for me, but I saw that there was hardly any where for me to sit.

I managed to squeeze in behind him on the side of the chaise. We sat and watched the sun set together. Sun sets on Molokai are like nowhere else in the world. The sun drops and you see a green flash as the sun disappears behind the edge of the ocean where sky and water meet.

Bill turned and put his arm around me, looked into my face and asked me if I was married. When I said no and he confirmed the same, he kissed me. There must have been spirits in the bushes because they shook. I was surprised and afraid of both the speed at which he seemed to be moving and the shaking bushes. I really didn't want to get involved again with someone now when I was moving to another Island.

Bill held me. He sensed my fear, so we just sat there for a long time watching the ocean as the stars came out, and the moon came up. Suddenly he got up and said "we go". We left and drove back in silence. Just watching the sky and feeling the wind in our faces.

When we arrived back at my condo, he got out and held me in his arms as he leaned against the car. I had never felt such spirit, power, gentleness, love, and protection in anyone's touch before. It was so comfortable and easy feeling in his arms. His chest was so massive; I was snuggled inside and felt safe. I felt the world had stopped when he held me. His arms completely enveloped me. I don't know how long we stood like that but time stood still. He released me and I went up the stairs, and inside. He simply said goodnight. No words were said, just feelings felt in spirit.

On the third day of meeting Bill Kapuni he called and said he would be over soon. He came around 3 o'clock p.m. We went over to the west end again....this time to Hale O' Lono (house of the shark) where the canoe races across the channel start for Oahu every fall. He told me about how he raced it, and they camped in pup tents the night before, and how he won the 4-man koa division. We leaned back in my little Toyota Echo car and watched the ocean and sunset.

Then, he told me that he had something to tell me! What shoe was he going to drop? He was not married but he had a woman living in his house. At which point I said, after being taken a back for a few seconds, that I was moving to Kauai and to call me when she is gone. We drove back to town and he wanted to sleep outside in Ili'i Park over night. He stopped at his A frame house and got pillows, blankets and sleeping bags. We slept in our clothes, under palm trees and talked very little.....mostly just looked at the stars, smelled and listened to the ocean and trades, and fell asleep.

When morning came, a horn beeped and woke us up. We gathered our things, got in the cars and went our separate directions. He understood what I had said and was dejected.

I had less than a week before I was to leave the Island. Bill called me every day two or three times. He found out my plans to go to the mainland to visit and move some of my things to Kauai and into storage. He strongly suggested that he go with me so that he could drive, and I could save my energy for my business and visiting my friends. He would be welcome also in the homes of my friends so we made plans for him to meet me in Kauai before we flew out for the mainland together. There was a few days were we could not speak because I did not have a phone.

He had, in our last phone conversation, told me the flight he would fly in on to Kauai to be able to join me in the flight to the mainland. I met the flight not really knowing if he would be on it or not. I waited at baggage claim and watched all the people from his flight come in and pick up their luggage. He wasn't among them. I felt sad and said to myself, I guess he couldn't make it. It wasn't meant to be. Before I turned to go to the car, I decided to walk up to the double glass doors where everyone had come from and look up the ramp to see if he was coming. If I left he wouldn't be able to find me with no phone.

I watched the open space behind the double glass doors for a few seconds hoping he would still walk down that ramp but doubting he would. In a few seconds, I saw him loping down the ramp towards the double doors. He saw me and flashed that huge smile that covered half his face, and we both realized how relieved and happy we were to see each other again. We embraced simply like friends do and he picked up his bag and we headed out into the air walking to the car.

I drove, and for the first time, I experienced a genuine back seat driver. He was terrible.

I am a good driver, with only two accidents, one backing out of the garage when I was learning how to drive at 16, and then I was rear ended once. At any rate, I had to get firm with this Hawaiian male and tell him to not open his mouth any more. He directed me to make some turns and asked me to pull over by the ocean at a boat harbor.

We got out and he leaned against the car and asked me to come to him. He put his arms around me and pulled me into him. He looked down at me and asked me "Will you marry me?" I was shocked and tongue tied for a moment. I said finally, "We don't know each other." He said looking straight into my eyes, "Yes, we do. We know each other in spirit and that's all we need." I believed him, but didn't give him an answer. I simply looked down and avoided his eyes. I was incredulous that this amazing man was asking me to marry him after only 3 days of actually seeing each other and a few days of talking on the phone.

This wasn't to be the last of it. I was to learn that when Bill Kapuni made up his mind and said something, that was it for he didn't make snap decisions. He took his time about making decisions; but when he decided something, what he said, was it -- the final word, because he always made his decisions with prayer in Spirit.

I had met Bill Kapuni in August, I found out he had lived 24 years in Washington state (the Pacific Northwest), and in July he had been sitting in his Bill Kapuni Snorkle and Dive Boat in slip number one while I was sitting watching the canoe regatta at the harbor. He told me he had sat in his boat and watched me sit there for quite a while with his two grand daughters! I had never seen him or noticed him nor felt him watching me. And we had both known each other before from the snorkeling trips… all like the fortune telling lady in the tree had predicted!

Bill the Hawaiian Gentleman

CHAPTER TWENTY-ONE

WHEN WE ARRIVED IN DENVER, IT was cold! We put on our warm coats and were still cold. Our Hawaiian blood was too thin for this rocky mountain fall. The wind was strong and biting at our faces. My hair was being whipped about by the wind and my ears were getting cold. Bill said, "It is going to snow". I hoped not, because I knew the roads we had to travel to get to Laramie, Wyoming at my friend's house were dangerous in snow and ice.

Route 287 was one of the most scenic roads in the country, but one of the most treacherous in a storm. I knew because I had traveled that road numerous times from Laramie to Denver and back. I had a near fatal accident, when I hit black ice along with trucks and other cars going down one of the hills at night. My car skidded under and back out from under a semi-truck as we slid down the hill together--I had no control whatsoever. The friend we were going to stay with lost two horses in her horse trailer on that road, when she also hit black ice. The night time was the worse time, and we were late afternoon heading into dusk.

Bill was an excellent driver in what turned out to be a bad winter storm with 4 inches, in an hour and a half, accumulated on the mountain roads as we hit them and more inches at the crest. He told me about his driving the State of Washington and Canadian roads to go skiing and how fast he drove from Seattle to San Francisco to stop his first love, Patty, from flying away to the east coast, because her parents didn't want her to marry him, a Hawaiian, even though she was carrying his child. Aside from loving her, it was a heartbreak for him, because he loved children and would never have any other biological children of his own. He raced to the airport to stop her but the plane had taken off. He was devastated and met his first wife, on the rebound. She was his wife for many years, and had died shortly before he revealed his pain to me on his boat during that snorkeling trip.

I felt very secure in the car with his driving. More secure then I had ever felt with anyone....including myself. You can tell a lot about a person from observing them when they drive, their focus, their coordination, and their confidence. I would later find out, he was extremely safety conscious and careful about everything, not just driving. I could feel safe with him; he had even been a body guard for the famous Hawaiian entertainer Don Ho.

My friend's ranch was a show place of Western Americana with its red horse training facility, wooden post circular corals, Frank Lloyd Wright looking ranch house, (that she designed) ranch hand bunk house, Little Laramie River running through the sections of ranch lands and lined with yellow aspen trees because it was fall and the area was experiencing one of its spectacular autumns. Indian summer it was called when the trees take on a frost, turn color and then because the weather turns warm again, hold on to the colored leaves for a few more weeks before shedding them.

That evening before turning in for bed, Bill held my hand, looked down at me, and asked me a second time to marry him. This time, I didn't answer either and looked down because I didn't want to see the disappointment in his face. It was all moving too fast for me, and we were visiting a place where I lived for 15 years of my life. It was filled with memories and I was emotionally finishing up a divorce. I was not very interested in getting involved with any new man in my life. By being logical and analytical, I was thinking with my head and not my heart.

Bill and I drove into town the next day as I had business to take care of. He did too, but what I didn't know. He called his daughter to tell her that the relationship he was in, was abusive and she had to get that woman out of his house before he returned home. His adopted daughter knew this and agreed to help. He was puzzled that she had never said anything to him when she knew he was being abused. He kept asking me why she hadn't brought it up. I told him. "I didn't know".

While at my friend's, we rode horses along the beautiful river running through her Ranch in and under the trees up its banks with the sun sparkling and the deep bright blue sky of Wyoming framing the golden aspen leaves on the trees. The crisp fall breeze brought forth the scent of musk, water, earth, and horses. It was nature's symphony of the river flowing over its rocks, the tree twigs snapping under the horses' hooves, saddles rubbing the horses as we walked, and the leaves tinkling like the sound of tiny symbols crashing in the fall winds.

The next morning, I took Bill to my favorite spot in Wyoming up in the Rockies by a lake called Marie. It is a glacial lake and is surrounded by pine trees and high granite peaks, called affectionately the Snowys, similar to the peaks of the Teton range but wider. We sat by the lake for quite a while absorbing the energy of the mountains. Bill picked up some stones and threw them in the lake skipping stones across the water. I stood up to walk some, but before I got more than fifteen feet away, he said, "Victoria", and I turned and he looked me straight in the eyes, and in earnest said, "will you marry me?" As he spoke, I looked at him for a long minute.

This was a place I would always let myself feel, and be relaxed. I took a breath and allowed my heart to speak for me this time. I said "Yes" and quickly added, "But I can't tell you when, maybe a year or so," I knew I had to be with him now.

Bill was so happy that he flashed a big smile at me, got up from the rock where he was sitting and came over to me, put his arms around me and kissed me full on the mouth. I didn't pull away like before. I had no fear this time. I was surrounded in his energy of love. Light encircled us spinning around as we clung to each other under the mountain tops. We were both quiet and content in our decision … so in spirit, in nature, in love. He was relaxed. I was nervous still yet, but sure I had made the right decision.

We made quite the couple when our hosts took us to dinner to celebrate our good news. My friend had known me through all my tribulations and was glad to see me happy at last. But the Laramie

Wyoming restaurant regulars had not seen too many tattooed Hawaiian warriors eating steak in their restaurant. My skin is so fair that we truly looked like chocolate and vanilla.

Bill and I at a restaurant in Laramie

Bill called home a few times along the way. He was making sure his female friend would be gone when he brought home his new fiancé. I didn't realize until much later what a shock all of this was going to be to all the people on his Island. They all knew him and knew that he had been with this other woman for a few years. Because they had shared a house, the people assumed they were married. Hawaiian culture allows for acceptance of a quasi marriage of a man and a woman living together as well as the right for the kane to tell the wahine to leave his house at any time and she must go. Now not only was she to be gone without ceremony, but he was bringing home a tall thin white woman with blond hair…angel hair he would call it.

We went to my storage units in Colorado to gather my belongings where we saw my ex-husband, and Bill told him about our intent to marry. They already knew each other from the two snorkeling trips we had made. Bill smoothed everything out so that it was not a difficult situation. He could do that with anyone who was of a reasonable nature and not filled with anger, hate and drama.

Bill was clear on when he wanted to marry. January was his birthday month and he wanted to have a wedding in that month so he could celebrate all good events in the same month.

Upon returning home, Bill moved into my condo knowing we were going to marry soon. He used to smile and shake his head how in all his adult life, before meeting me and moving into my condo, he had worked every day for some period of time on an art project of some type with wood, metal, bone something. He was simply amazed that it took him over four months to start up work again. We used to laugh and smile about it... imagine, at our ages we were so much in love. There was no question that for each of us, we had never been happier, nor ever had a better relationship. We both knew the reason, of course, and it was that we lived in spirit together.

CHAPTER TWENTY-TWO

IN THE 1980'S, SPANISH VISIONARY ARTIST, Rafael Trenor, was in his studio absorbed in sculpting a symbol for the 1992 Sevilla Expo. As he stared through the early morning beams of light, he was filled with an inner vision that would change his perception of reality. He followed synchronistic threads of geology, sacred geometry and mythology to see the sacred union between Earth and Sky, Mother and father, Gaia and Uranus, symbolized in geometry by the Cube and the Sphere. The two together represent universal wholeness bringing balance and harmony to the world.

He explained that "one day I read Plato's Timaeus where the elements of Earth and Fire are symbolized in geometry by the cube and the pyramid, the basis of the harmony of the soul of the world."

He planned a sculptural work that would involve 'excavating' the 8 corners or vertices of the cube. Each of these vertexes would be a tetrahedron, a three-sided pyramid and the cube would have to be oriented so that all the eight vertices would be above land. Since 70% of the earth is covered by water, there is only one possible combination that would allow all eight corners to be uncovered on land. Those eight sites would put a vertex on an Island in each of the three oceans and in five continents that comprise the earth's surface. The vertices would be opened in New Zealand (Oceana), Santiago de Compestela, Spain (Europe), the Kalahari Desert (Africa), Terra del Fuego, Argentina (South America), Baikal, Russia in (Asia), the Cocos Islands (Indian Ocean), the Corn Islands (Atlantic Ocean), and Molokai, Hawaii (Pacific Ocean.)

Bill, sculptor and carver of ancient style Pahu drums and ocean voyaging canoes had been awarded Lot #144, almost five acres of Hawaiian Homelands almost twenty years earlier. When he first walked his land which had been zoned agricultural, he laughed. It was a hilly area of Kalamaula Mauka full of stones and large rocks. He couldn't imagine being able to grow anything there.

He invited a Kahuna who reads rocks to see his land. She told him "Something is going to happen here, something big and nice." Bill replied, "Something big and nice would be rain!" Kalama'ula hadn't seen any rain to speak of for many years.

Rafael decided to visit Molokai through divine guidance but without a plan. When several of Molokai's Kapuna (wisdom keepers) heard what he wanted to do, they directed him to Bill. Rafael told him that he was looking for rocks to carve into a pyramid. "Well," said Bill. "I have a lot of large rocks, but you can't carve them, because to Hawaiians, rocks are sacred and alive."

Bill took Rafael to his land on the new moon. After blessings, prayers and chanting, Bill found the right pohaku, (rock) to use for the vertex. They spent the night near it and Bill taught Rafael about the various amakua (guardian spirits) protecting this sacred land. By morning Bill had his answer. The project would be accepted by the amakua and by the land. The tetrahedron pyramid would be built upon a very large pohaku, which a kahuna dreamed about a few nights later and was told to name it Ke'opuaolani, the name of the sacred wife of Kamehameha I. Ke'opuaolani had lived for some time in Kalama'ula, and Bill told me she was buried there on his land. It is said that King Kamahemeha had to crawl on his hands and knees and beg her to marry him because she was of the purest royal bloodline existing in the Hawaiian Islands.

Bill offered Rafael his aina, for the Hawaiian corner of The Soul of the World and assured him, "I will take care of it." -- an ancient promise stemming from his ancestors and to be kept through eternity.

They co-created the Pyramid over the pohaku named Ke'opuaolani. Over it, Bill constructed a wood framed pyramid, filled inside it other rocks and material excavated from the ground surrounding it, and covered it all with wire so he could place cement over it. Bill chose the color for the cement…a gold/bronze color. The first corner of the cube directly connects Molokai with three other corners of the cube….New Zealand, Russia, and Nicaragua through the lay lines of the cube visualized inside the earth.

In David Malo's book Hawaiian Antiquities, in the genealogy called Puanue it is said that the Hawaiian Islands, 'were actually formed from the corners of the earth and sky'. Is it a coincidence that this Molokai pyramid, visualized centuries later by a Spaniard, from half way around the world, co-created with a Hawaiian the first of eight corners of earth and sky…the Soul of the World the first global sculpture?

Soul of the World

Although I felt the power by the Pyramid and Vertex on Bill's land that first night we met, I didn't really understand its significance until much later. He told me he was scheduled to go to New Zealand for the WIPCE (World Indigenous People's Conference for Education) at the University of New Zealand. He wanted me to go and he wanted to take a side trip to open the vertex for the New Zealand corner of the world. I didn't really understand what that would mean, but I was to the point that wherever he wanted I supported.

I was surprised that when he was with his Hawaiians he was less affectionate with me in front of them than he was in front of strangers. I didn't understand that. I assume he had an image with them to maintain, and they certainly weren't used to seeing him affectionate in public before.

He was Mr. Aloha to everyone, and lots of people, in particular women, touched him. I didn't like it so I explained to him that he was giving away his mana by allowing that to happen. He understood, learned how to keep people at a distance, stopped to respect my feelings and protect his mana. I wanted him to protect his private space and energy. It was as if he had no private space. If you give Aloha to everyone equally, you treat no one special, and I was about to become special to him…his wife.

We had a disagreement about that because he told me to be aloha to everyone also. With my puritan ethics, I felt that if I was insincere about how I felt about someone, I was not pono with myself maintaining harmony and balance within.

Bill is charismatic for both men and women. He carried such powerful male energy tempered by the gentleness of being Hawaiian. It was amazing for me to watch. Sometimes I'd just fade into the background and watch how people interacted with and responded to him. Although he always watched me if we were separated by more than a few feet from each other, people were drawn into his energy like a magnet for he was much larger then life. I would just watch and hardly be able to believe he loved and chose me after 3 days.

During this trip I learned about this unique amazing man who had pursued me so hard and loved me so deeply. I made sure he absorbed all this new information about how you hold your wife dearest, (and put it into practice). People must have noticed a change in his wandering eye because I remember someone saying, "he was never really ready for marriage before you".

The truth was I don't think I had ever truly been ready to give myself to someone as a partner for eternity. I hadn't understood love in the way I was experiencing it with Bill. For once I had a man who loved and took care of me as much as I did him. I was not the only giver in this marriage. I was a receiver also.

Bill often told me I taught him about love -- what it really means between two people. I might have taught him about unconditional love because that is what I felt for him. With the exception of my biological son, my grandson, my Dad and my Grandmother, it was not something I had experienced before. We loved one another without anger and blame or placing conditions on each other for receiving love. This was the love I had read about in self-help books when I was suffering through my earlier marriages. I think in the very beginning we were aware on some level that we had to live each day with each other to the fullest. We recognized the rare occurrence of our meeting and our love for each other.

On this trip, we also started learning each other's cultures. He made sure I learned about his quickly like not speaking to any males (he called them mens) unless he was with me and not until the male spoke to me first. Bill had a difficult time understanding that women in my culture had male friends; especially professional women like me. I understood his point of view and culture, particularly given his sensitivity to previous unfaithful women in his life, and complied with his wishes.

Eventually, after watching me from afar he trusted my commitment to him only and likewise, I trusted his commitment to me only. He used to say 'eyes only for you'. Sometimes he would mix it up with the James Bond movie "for your eyes only," but then again he chose his words carefully.

He continued to learn about, understand and see my culture; because, after all, we were to be in a marriage blending two cultures. I was in Hawaii and respected and followed him; however, all the while he was learning and respecting my culture also. Our marriage was a mutual respect and love of everything about the other. If not loving everything about the other, then at least accepting it as part of that person in your love for them.

Bill attracted so much attention wherever we went. He enjoyed indigenous people, "particularly carvers", He was linked to them and they knew it. He knew so many people from across the Hawaiian Islands and New Zealand that had come to this conference, and he knew the indigenous carvers and hung out at the New Zealand carvers' booth. He worked on a piece of jade that someone had traded him. It was to be a shark…his amakua; and he intended to wear it at our wedding.

Bill wanted to dedicate the New Zealand point of the Soul of the World art project and we needed to go to South Island to do that. It was exciting that I was going to share this sacred mission with him. He treated me as a Spiritual equal.

All we had were the coordinates of where the cube should be. Bill wanted to dedicate and bless the land for the project so that until such time as the pyramid could be built there, the land would be protected for that purpose and the energy would be released to begin the process of universal wholeness of the earth. I left Bill with the carvers and went into the library in search for information as to where we should go to find the NZ corner of the cube.

We left the conference and traveled through spectacular scenery from Hamilton towards the airport in Rotorua through country roads, breathtaking farms of rolling hills blanketed with green grass, the color of which I had never seen before, with mountains in the backdrop. Some farms had sheep on them and we laughed at two buildings that were 'sculpted' into a sheep and pig. The scenery in New Zealand is stunning. Upon our return, Bill told a developer from New Zealand, who was trying to develop La'au Point on Molokai, why don't you stay in New Zealand? It is beautiful there and there is plenty of land. The developer didn't like the comment, but that's the way Bill was. He spoke his mind.

In Whakarewarewa, NZ, within the ancient majestic forest of trees, we visited a primordial area, whose endurance and timelessness in the realm of nature is beyond comprehension. Only a spiritual energy connection with them can comprehend these ancient beings of life. With nature you can open up your heart, and it never hurts you. You can be vulnerable without fear. That is one reason I am attached to Nature.

Bill and I eating dessert at an inn near our
sleeping quarters in New Zealand

CHAPTER TWENTY-THREE

WE MADE OUR WAY TO THE South Island and were met with open arms, because Bill always connected to the mana of indigenous people and had two to three people helping us locate the maps we needed. Bill purchased a Silva Classic Base Plate compass along with a ruler and protractor for him to work with the maps. In the meantime, he had a wonderful time talking to everyone in the map store and setting up contacts for a helicopter pilot to fly us to the point for a prayerful dedication. He got the name of a pilot or two, who would take us within the Park boundaries for the ceremony. One was off Island for a few days, but would be back. There was a strong storm coming over the 'Alps' of New Zealand now and it would be difficult to fly for a few days anyway. During Bill's conversations about the project, he was referred to a couple living near New Castle.

The Castle Hill area is named for an array of natural very large grey rocks protruding from the ground on a hillside. I made the walk up and around the rocks. (Bill was unable) I can say it was a spiritual place, of solemn solitude, where I felt great peacefulness. I sat at the base of a very large rock about 20 or more feet high and rested in meditation. I sat and watched my handsome husband to be leaning against a wooden fence watching me and waiting for me to come back.

Upon arriving at the contact's house, we learned they had changed our plans. For some reason the contacts in Castle Hill had become controlling about things and had called our helicopter pilots, who were now afraid to enter the park boundary without permits for the stop and dedication of the rock Bill would etch. They wanted to make a 'trek' in by foot (which would be impossible for Bill to do) in the right season...not now when we were there. Bill was not pleased. They did not know about lay lines of the cube project and Bill did not divulge that information to him. After all, the Hawaiian Soul of the World was also on a lay line of the cube. Rafael himself had done the lay line of the cube for Hawaii dedication and Bill was about to do it for New Zealand. The South American point south of Usaia was now under water and had to be modified by a lay line also. That pyramid had been dedicated as a National Cultural Monument for Argentina. It sits on a rock on the beach as the ocean tides move past it.

These contacts wanted us to take from the Castle Hill area a limestone rock which Bill helped saw to make a smaller more manageable piece for the drop dedication, if we were going to be able to do it at all now. We took this rock with us and headed for Arthur's pass where we could see Mt. Rolleston. We actually stopped at the café there and Bill was the center of attraction as usual. We picked up many more names of contacts at Arthur's Pass Store for helicopter pilots. Of particular importance, we purchased a three segmented and elongated postcard panorama of the whole mountain range.

We pressed on to reach Greymouth where we were to meet a friend. We stayed in the Bela Vista Motel, and our friend came at 9:30 am to pick us up for breakfast the next morning. We chatted about the rock and dropping the rock for dedication of the New Zealand corner of the Soul of the World. He too thought we would have no trouble getting a chopper pilot to take us to the mountain for dedication.

Of particular interest was our friend's story of two pyramids 3000 miles apart from each other. Each the exact type of stone, size, height and weight and width as the other. One was very near Greymouth on South Island and protected by the government. It was very difficult to get to see, but he knew exactly where the pyramid is located. He also told us of the difficult times now with escalated fighting over the dwindling supply of rare rocks being found.

He was 23rd generation of Easter Island people who were the third group of people in New Zealand thousands of years before. We went to his shop because he thought there was there a rock for Bill to use for the dedication. He had a beautiful rock that was perfect. It weighed 24 lbs, was black Adulite (scientific name norite). Glacial scrapes and half moon shaped marks were on it. It was 120 million years old from the first glacial period. He said it will last a long time and not disintegrate.

Bill started to etch on the rock to be used in the dedication of the point. He would carve the three intersecting lines of the top of the pyramid, write "Soul of the World, Vertex NZ, 2005 Bill Kapuni" with a korn for new beginnings etched after his name. Our friend gave Bill, to use while carving it, special water gathered from a sacred Lake at the headwaters of Ahaura River which is the spiritual home of all stones found in New Zealand. After Bill finished, he asked us to take a white scarf belonging to a friend of his—a Tibetan Monk—with us and place it around the rock at the dedication point on the mountain.

He was a most spiritual man, and we felt very close to him. He gave me three healing stones that evening as we departed: one long greenstone earring known in his culture to be worn by a healer. He recognized me as a healer. The second stone was a Labradorite from Labrador known as the only existing self cleansing stone. The third stone he cut for me and placed on a pendant tie for me to wear. It was a beautiful bright turquoise with white/grey markings and was extremely rare. As far as he knew the only pieces left in the world were the ones in his bucket.

The next day, we picked him up for breakfast. He had finished the two pieces we had asked him to make for us. They were truly stunning....figure 8s carved from the same green stone. For the Maori the 8 signifies a bonding of friendship, two lives becoming one for all eternity.

The breakfast was interrupted by a disturbing phone call from our contact we left at Castle Hill, who now had further foiled our attempt to place the rock on the mountain. He had now involved the Department of Conservation and stopped our third pilot from wanting to take us up. He now wanted his children to walk it in and drop it getting a permit from the Department of Conservation and Park Service....more bureaucratic entanglement. But more importantly he lacked the understanding of the spiritual significance and ceremony for the dedication. We were being blocked once again. As we both knew then, we were to turn in another direction. We were not angry. We both knew too well that it was meant to happen as it was unfolding.

Throughout the day we were engulfed with horrible rains from that severe storm that had moved into the coast, so we stopped in Hokitika, which for hundreds of years was a center of and recognized by the Maori as the source of pounamu (greenstone NZ) especially by the Arahura River which found the ocean on the coast just north of Hokitika. The Maori traveled throughout this portion of the country trading for pounamu, and as a matter of fact, South Island takes one of it's Maori names Te Wahi Pounamu from the stone. Ngai Tahu is the tribe vested with guardianship over the greenstone, and the people of this area of the West Coast are known as Poutini Ngai Tahu.

We finally reached Franz Joseph (the glacier we thought we were going to place the rock in) and stayed in a log tree house at the Rainforest Hotel. About 9:00 pm we started powerful prayers for the rock to be placed where it was needed to be placed for the dedication of the New Zealand point of the cube. Our friend had given me a rock, a green stone which was filled with tiny triangles representing the Vertex pyramids and made out of schist. We had collected quite an array of items from New Zealand: a healing stone from Labrador called I believe Labradorite, the two 8 configured green stones he had carved for us from the same stone, the bone weapon the Maori carvers had given Bill in the North Island, four green stone adse he had given Bill for carving (they came from Canada), the jade earring, a turquoise and grey stone pendant, the 120 million year old glacier rock for the point of the dedication, a large jade shark pedant (half carved), and a green stone with schist triangles embedded in it.

Bill placed the three elongated and attached postcards of Arthur's Pass behind our treasures from the earth received from New Zealand, and then placed some ferns, from the beautiful rain forest we were in, behind all of that, his red and yellow kihe he had brought on the trip. The kihe is a sacred Hawaiian garment worn during ceremonies.

We used his red and yellow kihe worn only by Ali'i (royalty) for our pule. We not only prayed for the Vertex dedication but in particular prayed for the storm to clear out of the area so the helicopter could take flight up the mountains.

When the weather broke, Bill obtained clearance from the pilots to bury the rock. As we approached the beginning of the relatively small sculpted indentations on the mountain rocks filled with snow, the clouds began to roll in over the tip top of the mountains and closed in on us as we were approaching a landing on Franz Joseph Glacier. The pilots were forced to quickly maneuver the helicopter around and speed back in retreat of the visibility problem fast approaching us. We were heart sick to have gotten so close when we returned to the landing site.

We traveled down to the town named Fox Glacier in very rainy weather...it seemed to be getting worse. The Fox Glacier helicopter flight line was closed for the day due to inclement weather. Dejected and proceeding in the driving rain, once again turned back on our plans, we found a turn off to Gillespie's Beach where we went and discovered the beach is made of stones! (Gillespie is my maiden name.) It was a rocky beach! As we lived our lives, everything happens for a reason, we delighted in walking through the stones and collecting many. Right by the ocean, the rain had stopped, but when we returned to the highway, there it was again.

We were trying to get to a helicopter that would take us up to the mountain. The pilots at Franz Joseph told us to head over towards the Mt Cook area where the weather was influenced differently (being inland) than the west coast weather. So we proceeded driving in the rain down to Haast Village where we saw another wonderful beach laidened with more rocks and tree stumps! Hundreds of tree stumps! We both felt at home with the pohaku and ocean. The beach had a river and large hill going into the ocean which interested us. We splashed and played in the river as it traversed the beach. All the while, we knew our journey was being directed and meant to happen the way it was. One simply must remain humble and trust that all happens for a reason.

Our voyage took us through "Lord of the Rings" country, Lake Wenuka and Lake Hawea, New Zealand. The aina just became more and more amazing to us. The Alpine mosses and grasses were in rich earth tones. The land was surreal and diverse and the mountains were more jagged because New Zealand is a relatively newer land mass where wind and water erosion has not had as long a time to have their way with the aina. The hills and mountains are steeper, delicately sculpted, less rounded and more dramatic then we were used to.

That evening we decided to 'let go' and not try so hard to get our mission accomplished and pray again and believe that if it was meant to happen and we were meant to bury the 120 million year glacier stone, we would. We felt like we had been hitting our heads against a wall trying to get the second Vertex dedicated at every turn with the pilots and weather. We were just grateful to be out of the rain and turning the whole situation over to Ke Akua (God), who would make it happen if it was supposed to happen.

Having turned the responsibility of dedicating the point to prayer, we slept very well, indeed. The view from the Inn was spectacularly peaceful complementing our restful states of mind. As we left this serene setting, we gazed at fields of lupine marching into the lake and felt we would place the rock today because the skies were crystal clear—not even one cloud in the sky when we awoke. We journeyed to Wanaka and through the beautiful country marveling at the great variety, and stunning beauty of this majestic land once again.

Soon we came upon Twizel and then onto Glentanner Park were we were to catch a helicopter to the mountains. We arrived prior to noon, but missed our 1:00 p.m. flight and waited for the 1:30 p.m. one. The 1:00 p.m. flight went to where Bill thought the lay line was and the 1:30 p.m. flight did not.

Bill had me hold his backpack while he entered the copter. I noticed how light it was compared to how heavy it had been for the Franz Joseph flight. We actually left at 1:45 pm (15 minutes late) instead of 1:30 pm., because of the inclement weather. Bill had made sure with the pilot before hand that he could leave the rock at the landing sight. "No problem." As a matter of fact the pilot took our picture at the top landing spot holding the rock. We were accompanied by two Japanese, who didn't speak much English, but they took our picture also.

The amazing circumstance was that because we left 15 minutes late and because of cloudy weather, this 1:30 pm flight changed its' flight pattern abruptly and landed at the very same landing spot Bill had chosen for us on the 1:00 pm flight we had missed!

We believe the lay line runs from this landing place close to Mt. Rolleston, through Arthur's Pass, through the land mass forming a 'v' in the northern part of South Island near Mapua and a larger place, Nelson, but then through the North Island and on to Molokai, Hawaii.

Bill, after prayers, buried the rock in the snow at approximately 2:00 pm December 7, 2005 New Zealand time in two feet of snow. The spiritual dedication had been completed. The rock went into a two foot hole Bill had dug in the snow. We felt spirit surround us on that mountain top kneeling in the snow together in silent prayer.

We were in spirit…we had experienced something sacred together. I had a Spiritual partner at last.

We are dedicating the New Zealand
Point of Soul Of The World

CHAPTER TWENTY-FOUR

Even before our arrival home, on the plane, Bill drew for our wedding the plan for the hall, stage and outside on a piece of paper. I didn't know that he had had a thriving business of running luaus for tourists. He knew exactly what he wanted because it was important for him to have a traditional Hawaiian wedding so he could introduce me to his people properly. He did not skip a detail. He even had a place for us to display our respective artwork. He designed walls of coconut tree branches made to enclose the outside area.

While we were shopping for the wedding, we ran into one of Bill's friends, whose band later played for us at the wedding. Upon hearing our news, he grinned and asked me, "How much do you know about this guy? Do you really know what you are getting into?" Bill gave him a look and he said no more, and I didn't ask. I realized later that the man was referring to Bill's well-known controversy and activism. Had I known that, I would have really felt at ease. I didn't know at the time that I would be playing an instrumental role later of protecting Molokai as an activist myself.

We needed to look for a dress for me and find a shirt maker to make him a white shirt and a red sash and white pants for what he had decided to wear. It would be billowy sleeves gathered off the shoulder, like a pirate's shirt, mandarin collar, and open at the neck. The sash had to be red...and of course very long.

He wanted a very Hawaiian wedding so I looked for a Hawaiian dress. He watched me try on every dress and helped pick out what I should try on, and he didn't like any of them. We finally went to a traditional wedding dress shop and I tried on three gowns. He really liked one so I ordered it to be made to fit my tall body.

It was very beautiful and white, which I questioned because white is usually reserved for your first marriage ceremony, but after talking to people, the suggestion was 'wear what you want'. We both felt as if it was our first marriage, so I thought white would be fine. It was a simple V-neck with plain fabric material going over the shoulder to a V in the back, where at that point, there were covered buttons going down the center of my back to my leg at which point the skirt flared and draped to a slightly billowed train trailing on the ground about a foot. The bodice was tightly fitted until just below the waist and then it flared out to a wide A-line skirt. The front and back were trimmed in delicate beading. I felt like a new blushing bride…like the first time should have been.

I felt that this was, indeed, the man of my life, the one I should have married the first time. I was more nervous then my other weddings and attributed that to the feeling that this was it…my husband for eternity, as he was fond of saying to me.

We had each waited to find the other during our whole lives. When we chose the date only four months after our first kiss, he said "why wait?" We are adults and know what we want. He was right. In retrospect, I think he simply wanted to make up the time lost in our lives of not being together.

Bill had carved a figure 8 pendent for me out of a mother of pearl shell, and purchased a Tahitian black pearl on one of our trips to Kauai to glue in the center of the larger lower circle of the figure eight. I would wear this on my wedding day.

We made so many plans for a wedding that would suit what I saw and I think others saw as a king of the Island taking his bride. At the time, Bill was respected by many acolytes as their Kumu teacher of Kahuna ways and I don't think they believed that I understood Bill's strength, abilities and Mana.

They just saw me as a haole (foreigner) from the mainland. They didn't know me at all, for I had one of his students ask me if I knew he was a Kahuna! I politely nodded, but realized how important he had been to these people. I am not sure they understood the connection we had, and I sensed some jealousy as they perceived that I was stealing away their leader.

We were lost in our love for each other. His close friends made it a point of telling me that they had never seen him so happy. Certainly my friends, the few who were able to come in from the mainland for the wedding, could not believe the change in me. I was now walking three feet off the ground at all times. I was so filled with joy and love, that my smile radiated -- only to be matched by Bill's.

We prepared a wedding with no detail unnoticed. If Bill wanted it we did it. I felt like his queen and loved that he took charge. We had over four hundred people to the sit down luau with table decorations of ribbons, candles, and sparkling glitter to catch your eye and match the floral table settings of orchids, ferns, birds of paradise, and ginger. A friend of his went to the mountains for the korn fern because in New Zealand it represents new life and harmony for us on our new beginnings as husband and wife.

We had the most beautiful four tiered cake with butter cream icing covered with real red roses and baby's breath. One band played Hawaiian standards and the other played vintage 'oldies' from our time. We got beautiful matching dresses for Bill's little grand daughters, one would be the flower girl and one the ring bearer.

When we were getting tired making all the arrangements we took his family out for dinner for Bill's birthday. It bothered Bill that his son-in-law never showed, but I really didn't think much of it at the time.

One week before our big day, Bill said let's go to the east end today. His plan was for us to go deep into our spiritual life, to pray and be with Loni Kaula. I went into my meditation as always when I was close to the area, and Bill, after asking permission, drove through the fence into the area.

This time, we walked to a different side of the stand of kakui nut trees to the west side across tall grass about three feet high. Normally, I would be afraid to walk through grass of that height, but with Bill I was never afraid anywhere of anything. I went to one tree and touched it and walked around it stopping at one side and simply bowing my head and touching it with my forehead and both hands.

Bill went off into the middle of the grove and returned later and said, "He wants to marry us". I said, "Who wants to marry us?" He said, "Loni Kaula". He began to look for nuts and rocks to smash open the nuts with. It seemed to me he was crashing around in the trees with his blue and white bandana on, black shorts, old white tee shirt (his usual uniform) making noise. I don't remember what I was wearing but I know I had shorts on because of the tall grass brushing my legs.

We were being raised higher and higher in spirit. Our eyes were bright and glowing and we were walking off the ground. While he was breaking the nuts and I was standing there watching him, a very large kukui leaf fell on my head and brushed down the side of my hair and down to my feet. I told Bill and he said, "He's playing with you." I said "Who is?" With a big smile, he said, "Loni Kaula is playing with you". By that time, he had some nuts cracked open, how I don't know, because they are so hard to open, but we took the little cups of nuts filled with liquid (Kukui oil). Bill said, "He wants us to drink with him", and so we did. Bill said, "He has married us now". We kissed and held each other a long time in love and in spirit under the kukui nut leaves rustlings above us.

Our drive home was quiet as we held hands in the car as we almost always did. He would take my left hand and hold it on his leg as he drove sometimes rubbing it and sometimes just holding it, but always taking it onto his leg. We were in peace, light and the knowledge that we were married in spirit now, and nothing would or could ever change that. What joy and comfort we felt to know we were already married.

This was all meant to be, because although we never fought before, the following day we had a fight over what I do not remember or care for that matter. It might have been jitters. I know that part of me was still nervous about marrying a man from a completely different culture, whom I had known for only a few months.

I left the house because I didn't like to fight and drove away ending up on Bill's homestead land. Aside from the Soul of the World Pyramid he also has a medicine wheel that was made with the help of a Hopi Indian, who came to visit Molokai and found Bill. The Hopi had assisted Bill with his first wife's death. When I got to the land I entered the circle of rocks forming the medicine wheel for answers.

Medicine Wheel overlooking the balcony
of our home on Molokai

Indian tribes always camped in a circle and always sat in a circle. The Hawaiians always sat in a circle for awa ceremonies. There was always a center to the circles. Indians do everything in a circle because they believe the power of the world always works in circles and everything tries to be round. There are four directions within the Medicine Wheel. Indian people were strong and happy as long as the circle was unbroken for it was nourished by the four directions: the east gave peace and light; the south gave bountiful blessings for warmth to nurture and grow everything; the west gave us rain and a courageous adventurous spirit; and the north with its wind and cold gave us strength and endurance.

I walked it and entered spirit and first asked for his first wife to listen to what she had to say about Bill. I was very satisfied with her answer and then asked Spirit what I should do about the wedding. No answer. I asked then if I should marry him? The answer was loud and clear… "You already are married!"

With that answer, I returned home to find he had packed up all his clothes in his suitcases and they were at the door. He said someone was coming to pick him up. I was shocked and sat down to talk. I went into the discussion with him and shared with him what I had heard at the medicine wheel -- what Spirit had told me -- we were already married! He acknowledged that with a smile and said he knew we were already married in spirit also, and he unpacked. We hung up his clothes together.

Later on in our relationship after our wedding, I asked him why he had done all that. He replied, "I just wanted to see what you would do."

I felt blessed that some of my mainland friends and family had been able to make such a long and expensive trip, because I was in need of people around me to help me stay focused and grounded. Bill was very busy with all the 'male job workers,' and I was drifting around marveling at all the work that was being done on our behalf by so many local people I didn't even know.

My hairdresser first did my matron of honor's hair, and she came out looking like Marie Antoinette. She stared and stared at herself in the mirror in disbelief. She, being a rancher, never got her hair done up like this and she was surprised to see what she looked like this way. She actually liked it and couldn't stop staring at herself in the mirror. Then it was my turn. My friend made me feel beautiful with my hair brought up off my face and piled in back of my head in curls. In this traditional Hawaiian wedding I would be wearing no veil so she placed a feather lei -- a Lei Hulu -- around my head.

Bill and I both wore lei hulus. They were made out of goose feathers and dyed. In the olden days the Lei Hulus were made out of bird feathers but those birds are not around anymore so now the goose feathers or duck feathers are used and need to be dyed to mimic the bird colors. Mine was a dark and light green color for the colors of Molokai and his was yellow and red designating Ali'i colors. These lei hulus were round and had been made by hand. It is a long process of cleaning cutting and tying every single feather into the lei hulu. They were intricately covered with feathers colored to make the design and tied with a ribbon at the ends to fasten around our heads.

Then my matron of honor and I were off to the house where we would have awa. We were late, of course, probably because girl things always take longer then you anticipate, and I was not used to having 'girl things'done to me. Everyone was waiting when we arrived. Bill particularly was a little anxious for my arrival and was waiting out ahead of everyone else. I went up to him and we hugged while he asked me where I had been.

Bill moved everyone out to the beach area where we all sat on the ground with Bill's friend, a Maui Kahu, (Hawaiian minister from Maui) who was to preside over the Awa Ceremony and the nuptials later. Bill likewise was a Kahu able to marry people. He had been an Ordained Minister of the International Assembly of Spiritual Healers and Earth Stewards Congregations.

We had met with an Awa Ceremony and we felt it appropriate to start our marriage with another one, symbolic of our new beginnings and celebrating that day we met in spirit. It was to only be us and the officiating Hawaiian Kahu and his assistant and the best man and matron of honor.

Several people had found out about this ceremony and followed Bill to this place and he gestured for them to join us. We were honored they wanted to join us. We were all in spirit together sharing our na'au (feeling from our core) and hearts. For a man of few words, Bill spoke a very long time about our spiritual lives together.

After the Awa Ceremony, we went in to get dressed. I remember I was the first one ready. That was always the way with Bill. I always finished dressing first. He was very meticulous about his appearance, and I was not. I emerged from the house first, and people smiled and sighed at how I looked; however, when Bill came out in his romantic hand made white shirt and white pants, red sash, and matching red and yellow lei hulu, everyone made a very loud 'ahh' sound and clapped ... so much more than for my appearance, I actually said, "How come you think he looks so much better than the bride?" That was the way of it with Bill. He was always the one who caught everyone's attention, because he was so tall, dark and handsome and had such a powerful presence. I didn't really mind because I was mesmerized by him as well.

Bill picked the wedding site for its Hawaiian significance and spirituality. When you approach the top of the cliff overlooking the ocean, if you are at all spiritually sensitive, you can't help but feel the iwi (bones) of the ancients. Bill said his best friend Eddie, who had drowned in the Molokai channel came ashore there also. I liked the space for its spiritual energy, and the beauty of the crashing waves upon the rocks. There was both a kane (male) missle rock and wahine (female) cresent moon shaped rock in the ocean just to the north of the small flat space of aina on the top of a sea cliff hillside where we were married.

Our Kahu officiated for our very Hawaiian wedding lacking only the portion of getting in the ocean wrapped only in our wedding tapa. Since we both knew we would be faithful to each other we did not feel the need for this portion of a Hawaiian ceremony created for the couple to keep themselves faithful only unto each other. The wedding tapa is the size of a bed spread. Lauhala leaves are pounded flat with wooden mallets like Papayrus paper made in Egypt, and then the tapa is hand painted. The artists who make them are mindful of prayer and being in a spiritual place when they pound the Lauhala to make the cloth, and paint it with Hawaiian designs in paint made into dyes from plants. As is with all Hawaiian creating, the process is a spiritual one, and done with aloha intention, honor and respect for the material, process, ancestors that came before, and the culture.

CHAPTER TWENTY-FIVE

Bill placing the maili lei on me during our wedding ceremony

ALTHOUGH IT HAD RAINED THE PREVIOUS fourteen days, the skies cleared for the day of our wedding and reception... the dawning of a new beginning for us. The procession, lead by Bill's granddaughters went past a hillside covered with the rare Kai Hina Hina hawaiian flower. We faced the ocean and large rocks as the Kahu began with a blowing of a Pu (large conch shell) and a Hawaiian Oli (prayer) Aloha chant, where he called the spirits of the Island to join in our joy, and they were responding. He translated one prayer into: "This is the sight for which I have longed. Now that you are here, love has come."

Kumu called us by our Hawaiian names throughout the ceremony at our request: Kuamo'o and Kulani. Bill had given me my Hawaiian name KuLani by taking parts of his name to create and form mine. The intent of the meaning by him for Kulani was Queen of Heaven he said.

Our Kahu continued by saying we had come to this place to make a new beginning for ourselves, and to make a commitment from this day forward to be husband and wife. We would commit ourselves to a life journey together and close all doors of the past to joyfully open the doors to our future together. We were to love one another as we had never before loved-- in spirit. I was no longer the wife of men who couldn't give to me. I was now with the one chosen for me … the one who deeply loved me like no other.

The next part of our Hawaiian ceremony was the Lei exchange. Hawaiians give leis as a gesture of welcome from each other, the aina and the ancestors. It is a ceremony of love. The giving of the lei symbolizes a giving of a part of ourselves. The special maile lei used for important ceremonies like a wedding is a lei of love and peace. It remains always open as a symbol of our openness and acceptance of each other forever.

We presented these leis to each other with a kiss. The love in this exchange was remarkable. His love for me was like none I had ever felt -- brimming with love, light, strength and protection. When he placed the maile lei on me, no one has ever looked at me with such deep love before.

Our Kahu did another chant calling iwi, aina, and ancestors and proceeded to the declaration of our intentions to love, cherish, respect each other, make each other our closest and dearest companion, commit to each other whole heartedly and Bill would give his strength and wisdom to support and comfort me. I knew I would be taken care of by my husband. He was a Hawaiian warrior who would protect and support me like no one in this world had ever done. We cherished each other. Cherish is a word I never used before to describe how I felt about a husband. Bill and I really cherished each other.

When the Kahu gave him the signal, Bill said to me "I Kuamo'o take you Kulani to be my wedded wife, to have and to hold from this day forward; to love and to cherish, to trust and respect; for better for worse, for richer, for poorer, in sickness and in health, and to live each day in the name of God forever and always." I said the same to him.

The blessing and exchanging of rings which symbolized Ke Akua' unending aloha and our unending aloha for each other followed. In the Kahu's blessing and pule, Bill said to me: "Kulani with this ring I promise to grow with you. To build our love. To speak openly and honestly. To live with you in spirit. To love and cherish you, for all the days ahead. From this day forward, you shall not walk alone. My heart will be your shelter and my arms will be your home. With this ring, I thee wed. I loved that part and said the same to him. His arms were my home and his heart was my shelter. They were from the moment we had held each other at Lake Marie.

We were told to go forth on our journey together comforting each other, sharing joys, consoling each other in sorrows, keeping each other regardless of the vicissitudes life may bring. We were told to trust each other, live life and not be afraid. He prayed for us to be given the gift of memory of this moment, day and place for the rest of our lives....and beyond.

"Those whom Ke Akua has joined together let no one separate."

Sealed with a Kiss

"You may seal your vows with a kiss." And we did…..people grew restless at the length, but we were in spirit and mindless of time. Finally the audience's restlessness, brought us out of spirit, and out of the kiss with their noise.

Me Dancing the Hula for my Husband

CHAPTER TWENTY-SIX

My Husband watching me dance the Hula

WE WALKED INTO A STANDING OVATION and applause at our reception; and after we sat down, people began the line of congratulations. What a happy time for us. Bill was just beaming. There was so much joy for us from the guests. Everyone was lifted by our great joy and love and became connected to us with that love. I didn't know many of the people, but I could see the love and reverence people had for him. I could also sense the family relationship people had with each other because on Molokai there is likely to be a family relationship between most people somewhere down the line.

We were so very high in spirit and off the ground. I had asked Bill to pay attention to me as I would feel insecure in front of all his many friends and to look at me when we danced. We had been practicing. He just had to say "Relax", and my fear would melt away in his arms.

When he looked into my eyes, I was held in his strength and felt safe, and was suspended in his energy and protected from everyone and everything. He had that effect on me. I had it on him also... at least calming him and later on holding him in my energy also. I brought peacefulness into his life, and he then could express his gentle nature to me. That was one of the things that made him so happy. He could be himself with me. His outer appearance was one of a powerful black belt Hawaiian warrior, his inner self was one of an artist. I learned from others that Bill could be a strong aggressive athletic man of tremendous power that no one wanted to mess with when he felt on the defensive and aggressive. He was never on the defensive with me. I never attacked him.

After the congratulations, Bill announced dinner would be served. He liked the old fashioned luau where everyone sat down and were served at the tables. He didn't like the newer way of standing in a buffet line and getting your food. We sat down and people enjoyed the ono (good) traditional Hawaiian Luau.

After the meal, we got up and danced. I took a deep breath as I entered his arms, but he looked into my eyes the entire time. I was lifted and supported by his gaze. It was just like our vows...his heart will be my shelter and his arms will be my home. The moon was full, the stars bright, and the trees sparkled from the thousands of tiny lights, the candles glowed from the tables. It was – magic!

The band played for their old friend, Bill. Turning and turning as we danced in our bare feet in the night air, gentle breeze, twirling and twirling, not seeing anyone but each other as we laughed and gazed into each other's eyes. We were alone in the universe. Magic as others joined us in dancing. We were blessed for that time and living in the moment. What a glorious happening it was!

The tradition for a Hawaiian wedding is for the bride to dance a hula for her husband. I wanted to please my cultured Hawaiian husband. I learned the best I could in two weeks and gave my heart to him through dance. He looked so in love, happy and proud of me as his wife, a white woman, dancing hula for him. To see his face of appreciation and love was everything to me. It was very special for me to do that for him. His brother, who knew this was a first time for Bill to be honored by his wife dancing hula for him at his wedding, cried openly.

Bill and I continued dancing and when others cut in to dance with the bride he quickly found a way to pull me back to him. We were transported in each other's arms and high in joy and spirit as the music played and the people danced around us.

I was so grateful for that wedding of weddings. People talked about it for weeks, and those who missed it told us that were sorry, because they heard how wonderful it was. It truly was a wedding to remember by everyone....especially us.

CHAPTER TWENTY-SEVEN

WE BEGAN OUR MARRIED LIFE EXTREMELY close in spirit, mind and body. Shortly after the wedding guests departed, a friend of mine asked me if Bill would gift a Pahu drum to four Molokai youth, who were going to represent Hawaii at the Art of Living Foundation as it celebrated its Silver Jubilee in Bangalore, India. They would use the drum while they danced hula at the Jubilee and then present it to His Holiness Sri Sri Rami Shanker. On Molokai, upon gifting the drum to our four Hawaiian representatives, Bill said the Pahu is a "voice we pass on in energy. The Hawaiians have always used the Pahu to communicate". We donated the Drum in the name of Soul of the World Foundation. (International Peace Art Project) for the world peace celebration in India.

Upon their return home, I learned how one of them was eventually able to gift the drum to his Holiness Sri Sri and once again saw how everything happens for a reason. The four Hawaiians were not able to return home on the day scheduled. Eventually, upon the day of their leaving, everyone else was gone from their dorm rooms when the last one to leave picked up the one remaining item in the room -- the pahu she had been unable to gift to Sri Sri.

She was thinking she might have to take it back home with her and then walked out the door and down the stairs. She was on the 3rd floor of one dorm building and descended the outside stairs to the second level and onto a ramp connecting her building with another building. She ended up right in front of a door which suddenly opened before her, and who should appear, without his usual entourage, but his Holiness Sri Sri by himself! This was all done in spirit, and she was able to approach him with the drum in her hands and give it to him – just the two of them in that moment on a landing outside the dorm room buildings. She gifted our Pahu drum from Soul of the World to his holiness Sri Sri Rami Shanker.

Bill and I just continued to float for months. He never got back to work until the beginning of April. And each day, we just hung around together and went to the pool and the beaches and talked and had a wonderful time with each other. We didn't watch TV and we didn't visit people. He said he had never been able to talk to anyone before like he was able to share with me. A lot of our communication was on a spiritual level about Spirit. We had evolved individually and now together we had ascended from a physical reality to a spiritual awareness not grounded in time and space. Even our sexual relationship was on a spiritual level and far more intense and important than in only the physical. Neither one of us had experienced anything like it before.

Bill lived with his tutu in a grass shack on the beach in Oahu when he was young; as a teenager, he became a member of the so called Honolulu Hobo Club living in box cars and taking care of other young boys doing the same. He was hanied (Hawaiian term for adoption) by a family, who met him when he was 19. They came to visit us after the wedding and were able for me to fill in some of the things Bill had experienced in his life. They also had film of him when he was young and so beautiful that I would never have had the courage to talk to him. I would have been too shy. He was both a surfer and man of the land. The photo of him, with the famous surfer Eddie Aikau and his brothers from back then, I can still hardly look at because he was so handsome.

Aikau brothers and Bill surfing North Shore

I was under the misconception that when everyone saw how happy we were they would accept us as a couple. I didn't realize that that was not the way of the Island. For many months we would have Bill's granddaughters over at least once a week to stay with Papa and Grama. We all loved it. What I didn't know (although I should have because she never said a word to me at our wedding) was that Bill's adopted daughter wasn't at all happy with our marriage. Typical behavior of a jealous daughter over her father's new wife; and when Bill made it clear that our marriage was solid and here to stay, she would no longer allow us to see her children. I think she had a hard time knowing that there was now someone else who was number one in his life as she had always been. It broke his heart to lose his connection with his grandchildren which I more than understood.

In the beginning for about a year and a half, Bill and I made efforts to bring her together with us, but then she would go and do something even more disrespectful to us. I had trouble getting past that terrible hate and anger she manifested in words and actions towards us. I would feel Bill's pain and get angry with her intent to hurt him. I didn't interfere, but I felt him and how disappointed he was in her and how much he hurt from her actions and her keeping his granddaughters from us.

It amazed me that she had been raised by him and never practiced the Hawaiian culture particularly avoiding what is considered the biggest tabu – to hurt someone (let alone intentionally). To be Hawaiian was to carry the seed of aloha from the culture. Hawaiians place tremendous value in respecting elders and ancestors. He alone, not his deceased wife, wanted her and adopted her and took care of her when she was a baby. He so loved children.

Finally, as the situation continued to deteriorate, some of my Hawaiian friends began to tell me 'you have no kuliana (responsibility) towards her now', and advised me to let it go. Bill did too. Enough was enough he said. We endured great pain from her and her actions (the pain being mostly from not seeing the grand children).

From my perspective and looking back, I can see that it was the way it was supposed to be. If she had not acted that way, Bill would never have seen the real adopted daughter he had; and we would, perhaps, not have been able to grow as close as we did; because we'd have to deal with her continual interrupting drama scenes and problems as he called them. At one point I suggested we get involved with her life and try and help her. His reply was "do you really want to get involved with all her problems?" I didn't answer him because I didn't want to get involved with her pilikia (trouble) either. That was his enough is enough pain talking. Enough humiliation, enough disrespect, enough drama!

Bill often said, as we watched old family movies and looked at old family pictures, "whatever happened to my daughter"? I wondered the same thing. He would say, "it must be her genes. She must have something in her genes to make her act that way". Later, he thought and would say she started changing when, her husband came into her life. That is when she started drinking. This was the biggest disappointment in his entire life….to see how she treated him and kept the grandchildren from us.

CHAPTER TWENTY-EIGHT

By MARCH I REALIZED BILL NEVER was going to be able to move to Kauai even for just a year as he said he would before we were married. His heart and mind and spirit were in Molokai. I had to call my friend, Puna, one day and tell her I would not be moving to Kauai. It was as if I had stabbed her for the silence she left on the phone. I made Bill get on the phone with her as they had been friends since teenage years on Oahu, because I didn't want to feel her disappointment through the phone. Since it was his decision, I thought he should feel it, not me.

That's one thing I learned quickly, Hawaiians know each other either through personal friendships, family relationships or with friends of family or friends. They always went through their greeting conversations of how they were related or what knowledge they had of each other through various friends. For the non Native Hawaiian, it placed us outside the loop, but it was an important part of their relationships and their feeling of connectedness--of being Hawaiian. I have learned to do that now, also, as people connected to Kapuni start the connection conversation with me.

Puna and Bill were paddlers during similar time periods in Oahu. She took the news from him apparently better than from me. Puna was a little surprised we had gotten together, but she was glad to see that I was so happy. Later in our conversations through the years, she said I was on Molokai for Bill, although she recognized I had a relationship with the Island of Molokai long before I met Bill and told me so. For everything wonderful, mysterious and spiritual Bill is, I was brought here for him first and the Island second. He knew it also, for he would often say his tutu in Spirit would tell him to listen to me. And he would always follow what his Tutu told him to do.

I learned to be very relaxed swimming in the ocean on Molokai when I was with Bill. We took a visit to Kauai to see Puna and went into the beautiful turquoise ocean waters of the lovely Hanapepe beach in southern Kauai. We were swimming around and Bill was carrying me in the water like he does when he is not swimming. I felt so safe with him in the water and liked to be carried. I had talked to him about the likelihood of sharks and he said they didn't bother him much. He smiled and said "I only had to punch one once."

He also carried me on his back as he walked the sandy ocean floor which was also great fun for me. I laughed so much because I felt safe and was having so much fun in the water with him. He laughed because of how relaxed and happy I was.

He also liked to splash me in the water....just softly and gently so that there is a slight spray that reached me. We were having fun and there were people on the beach getting ready to come into the water...about 6 of them. He told me to walk away from him a few yards which I did. He then took off his bright red swim shorts with the white hibiscus pattern running down the side and threw them high in the air for me to catch.

Of course, all the tourists saw this and decided not to come in the water with us then! I'll never forget the grin on his face after he submerged himself underwater when he threw them and came up after I caught the shorts. He came out of the water to his waist and grinned like a bad boy getting away with something. I was shocked at what he had done and giggled a little. His coming out of the water after the deed was amazing ...like a Cheshire cat smile knowing he had scared the tourists away and had shocked his new wife.

He scared tourists away once at Halawa, where we would often go when we went to the east end of the Island. We would always go in the ocean together and I was not afraid even though the water was dark at the mouth of the river and sharks were said to be at the mouth of rivers joining oceans. Bill's amakua is a shark so he is never afraid of sharks. Some tourist came walking near us and Bill wanted to continue with our private swim and so he yelled at them...this beach is only for Hawaiians don't you know that? Even though I clearly didn't look Hawaiian, and it was not true, they weren't about to argue with the big tattooed Hawaiian male.

CHAPTER TWENTY-NINE

Bill FINALLY BEGAN WORKING WHEN WE returned to Molokai from Kauai, because he had two drums to do for the Maui Canoe Festival coming up in May and a commission to finish for Her Royal Highness Princess Abigail Kinoiki Kekaulike Kawananakoa three drums, which had been cut from a tree on her property; all of which he had started before he met me, and they had been sitting there waiting for him. It was an adjustment to have him working and not always with me. I remember when he first started leaving in the morning like a husband going off to work. I felt a real separation and we missed each other a lot. Bill called several times a day while he was gone just to stay connected even though we already were in mind and spirit.

Bill didn't like us separated and asked his daughter and her family to move out of his house where he had his workshop. She was twenty-six and it was time for her to leave the nest with her two children and husband. It was an old house, but after we fixed it up, we moved in and once again we were able to be together while he went to work in the shop. We were happy being together again all the time and even if we weren't in the same space, I could always look out the window or door and see him working. He even did some of his work up on the lanai so that we could be closer together still yet rather than him being all the way down stairs in his shop. We were funny. We just liked to be around each other's energy.

In April, I sold my condo we had been living in and we pooled resources so that we would have money to build a house on Bill's homestead land. When the plans were drawn, we included 20 foot ceilings to accommodate the height of his art work, and a structural plan to accommodate hurricanes of 150 mph winds to protect it. Since we were both artists we shared a desire for and appreciation of a beautiful home that would allow us to see the ocean, live outside and accommodate his big art pieces. At first we wanted a house big enough that we could include his daughter and her family. We wanted them in our lives. Bill's son in law, however, made it clear he did not want to live with us and the cost was prohibitive so we scaled down considerably and turned it into an artistic expression of ourselves.

While waiting for our home to be built we still "floated" around our temporary house, eating our breakfast together at sun rise on the lanai (outside porch/deck) and holding each other in our arms and living in our flow of energy. Bill was feeling pressure from the five drums, because we had been clinging to each other like teenagers in love for five months now, and he had not been working on them steadily. As he described it, each drum told him how it wanted to be carved, and the drums were calling him to work on them. The International Festival of Canoes, which was Maui's signature cultural heritage event in Lahina, honors and provides a link between indigenous peoples across the Pacific including master carvers from Marshall Islands, Cook Islands, New Zealand, Tahiti, Tonga, Palau, and Hawaii. Bill was invited to all but one of the festivals since its beginning in 1998. He was one of the main attractions and considered a legend.

Bill loved the camaraderie of the carvers. They were all spiritual men from various countries and their common interest was wood carving and canoes. The festival was two weeks long and viewers were able to watch the carving from tree to sea when the canoes were launched into the ocean. The carvers were paid for their work in cash and room and board. That was the nice perk…the fancy places to stay in and around Lahina and Ka'anapali.

Saturday before the completed canoes went into the water, there was a main street parade where all the carvers and their works were displayed on beautifully decorated floats. This was a parade I didn't want to miss…..like being a homecoming queen (which I had never been) riding with definitely the home coming King! Bill was anxious to have me sit on the float next to him before we even left Molokai for the festival. Unfortunately, I almost didn't make it.

CHAPTER THIRTY

WEDNESDAY, DURING THE WEEK WE WERE on Maui, I had an appointment with a dermatologist because I had had some skin difficulties. I had lived so many years in Arizona and the high Rockies, and Jersey shores during the summers while growing up near the sun and wanted to make sure everything was all right. One of Bill's former spiritual students, who I considered a friend, offered to take me over to Kihe for my appointment. Everything went well until we were traveling back to the festival in Lahaina. We came up to a light and the friend ended up in the right turn lane which she didn't want to be in, so she stopped and put her blinker on to get in the left lane. The problem was that the right lane was a continuous right hand turn lane and as we sat there, a large four wheel drive truck came barreling down on us apparently not noticing that she was stopped and ploughed into us.

Fortunately, the car we were in was a Volvo and fortunately I was wearing my seat belt. My head snapped forward at an angle (because I was looking at the line of traffic in the left hand lane) and back to a straight on position and forward straight on and back once again. My glasses flew off my head and when I stopped moving. I couldn't move because of the excruciating pain in my head. My driver got out of the car and talked to the other driver who came to the window to ask me if I was hurt. Without moving my head, I said I was and he called the police. An officer came, but my friend drove off before I could talk to the officer.

I started praying immediately when I was hit and all the way back to the festival. I held my head in place and messaged my neck blocking the head pain with my mind and praying. The friend dropped me off at the festival to be with Bill. I got out and attempted to walk down the sidewalk towards him. I kept veering off to the right side bumping into trees along the sidewalk and couldn't seem to make myself walk straight.

I believed I could and would, like all things in my life that were adversarial, grin and bare it, and move forward like an injured athlete—just shake it off. In addition, to my prayers, I was not choosing this reality of pain and injury. I was denying it as not real because it was not part of God. Bill noticed me coming and got up to meet me and to see what was the matter. He immediately closed up his work area and walked me, holding me up to walk straight along side him by placing his arm around my waist, back to the place we were staying which was just two blocks away.

We got to the room and I sat on the bed. Because my hand is sensitive to heat in a body when I heal signaling injury or disease, while holding my head, I could feel the heat from the injury. We both immediately started praying and I felt a little better and laid back on a few pillows. He was very concerned and argued with me about going to the hospital. I refused and just kept praying. I called my brother, also a Christian Scientist, and asked he and his girlfriend (a Christian Scientist) to pray with us also. "When two or more people are gathered in his name" the Bible says, I felt that prayers would be more powerful if they helped and joined us.

There was a very special carver's dinner that night and I wanted to go. I talked Bill into going in spite of his concern for me. It was the event of the year and I didn't want to miss it. When we arrived, Bill had to help me walk and as the night went on, I became worse and began falling down and he would have to catch me and literally hold me up to stand and walk. My lovely friend from New Zealand 'got in my face', as I was sitting down, and said, making me look in her eyes, "Victoria, you are in shock and need to go to hospital. You must go." She was such a good friend – one of those you meet during your life and there is an instant connection. I respected her but still didn't want to accept the injury as mine.

We left and went back to the room. After a short while, and observing me walk, Bill didn't listen to me anymore and just called an ambulance. Both he and the EMTs talked me into going to the hospital. They insisted. He stayed with me every minute except during the c-scan of my head.

In the emergency room I fell asleep and came upon this doorway with old, tall, wooden, doors and wooden framing, with about eight steps leading up to it. All the steps were curved around the portal doorway which had a rounded half moon porch where this large double door was centered. There were many people standing around and on the steps and people were behind me also. I did not recognize them except my mother was at the bottom step on the left side watching me, and my grandfather was on the right hand side. At the top in the double doorway standing in front of a golden glow was my grandmother, who looked at me sternly for a long moment not saying a word, but shut the double doors as if to say 'it's not your time yet...you have more to do'. All the people standing around faded away with the closing of the doors.

Whereupon I abruptly awoke, opened my eyes to see my husband's concerned face staring at me from above. I told him about the dream/vision and then the doctor came back and said I was bleeding on my brain and needed to stay the night. Bill stayed with me in intensive care sleeping on a chair. When he was with me, I was never afraid or alone. Most of the night, we prayed a lot.....he particularly. I tended to drift off to sleep always waking up with him looking at me or over me from above. But, I had no more dreams.

The next day when I awoke, a police officer came to finish his report on me and the injury. I was moved to a regular room because the bleeding had stopped now. Bill went with me, but when it was night time, they showed him out. I was very upset he was being made to leave. If I had had all of my faculties, I would have made a way for him to stay. I did the next day when I read their hospital policies and chastised the head nurse for sending him away last night.

The neuro-surgeon came in, and I told him I wanted to leave. He tried to persuade me to stay another day, but I wanted to be with Bill in the parade as the 'homecoming King and Queen'. I continued my prayers and not choosing this head injury reality that was trying to push in on my consciousness. I insisted on leaving, and because the bleeding had stopped, my brain didn't swell, and nothing else negative happened, he had to let me go. I knew something had changed in my brain, I just wanted to leave, be with Bill and in the parade. I called him at his friend's house and asked him to come and get me.

Before he came there were two nurses lined up to speak with me about healing and what had happened to me, what did Bill and I do to get me better to leave the hospital in two nights with a bleeding on the brain taking up a spot of one by one and a half inches shown on the x-ray? Before Bill came, I only had time to speak with one and simply gave him common sense advice about diet and exercise (nothing special). He was a young nurse with diabetes already. I maybe explained a little about the healing work Bill and I do, because that was what he was interested in, but I don't remember. I was so glad to see Bill after being separated about nine hours. We went back to the room again and I rested. So glad to be out of the hospital and with my husband again! I just rested and we prayed until the next day.

Saturday came and I insisted on going to the parade even though Bill was hesitant, but we both felt that the bleeding had stopped and if I took it easy I would be all right. The sponsors did a lovely job of decorating a pickup truck for us, and Bill and the drum were already on the truck. I thought, I'll just climb up and sit next to him. I was wrong. I tried and fell over the side of the truck as I attempted to climb up, because my legs didn't work as I intended them to. Someone came and lifted me up while Bill pulled me up inside the truck to sit next to him.

A gracious lady made me a special head band from hala leaves. There even was a rose on it! She felt that I needed something since Bill had a large head piece for his head. We rode in the parade and it was amazing with everyone waving and cheering for Bill. The two announcers at the two micro phone points introduced me as Bill Kapuni's new wife, Victoria. I was surprised he told them to do that. He directed all things around him. People simply did what he asked of them.

I loved this time of our life together. We were still timid of each other and in each other's energy with cultural differences between us in every way but faithfulness, loyalty, love, being pono (honest and balanced), speaking from the na'au (gut). Those were the same core values in our cultures and in our relationship. I remember in those early relationship and marriage days we even had language barriers and spent a great deal of time simply understanding each other's vocabulary. We would have to ask each other the meaning of a word the other had used.

2006 Maui Canoe Festival Parade

It was very special to be married to him. In some ways it was rather like being married to a King. I had watched the King and I so many times as a young girl with Yul Brenner and Debra Kerr. Their relationship was similar to Bill's and mine. From our two different cultures, we challenged each other's cultures and searched out ways to blend the two, and we did. I felt like her when they danced together in the movie and he put his hand out to place around her waist as she taught him how to dance in her culture.

I suppose looking back, that movie also influenced and showed me that a relationship between two cultures could be loving and exceedingly very rich. The movie ends with a song "when a man wants your love, needs your love, what a wonderful thing". I remembered those words, and that was the way it was with us.

Shortly after the parade there was an Awa Ceremony , and everyone went to the canoe launching area. Bill was the last to walk through the crowded pathway into the beach area. His drum was already in place with microphones placed at the bottom of it to pick up the sound better. He chanted and had me walk by his side a little behind him. He placed me next to him beside the drum while he was introduced and played the drum for the launching of the canoes. I remember the friend, who made me the head band, had tears streaming down her face as he played the drum; because the drum, the communication of Hawaiians, was made with so much of his spirit and it sang the song of Hawaii.

He insisted I stand beside him. That is something people didn't understand much about our relationship. He would say where he wanted me when we were in public -- sometimes even at home. We were so accustomed to what the other wanted, eventually no words were needed. We just knew. Usually he wanted me right by his side. "Stand by me" he'd say all the time until I automatically did it. That was probably because he loved my energy as much as I loved his. What I realized later was that he was starting to feel vulnerable when my energy was not there for protection... just as I felt vulnerable if he was not there beside me to protect me.

It was a curious thing for me to feel and understand. I never had that experience with any one before. Neither did he. All I can say is, that our relationship was a very special one. It wasn't that we weren't whole and complete without the other, it was just the joining of our energies was so special for us; and our lives were so private, we felt protected by the other when in public if we were next to each other. We were, after all, each other's warrior who protected the other from outside dark energies should they come towards either one of us. That is what he told me early on before we married: "in order to marry me, you have to be my warrior and I will be yours". Traditionally, only Molokai women fought alongside their men during the Island kingdom wars to care for them if they were injured and take their place if they were killed.

We left the festival and went home on the Molokai Ferry. The doctor had said I needed to get lots of bed rest, don't do anything strenuous (even making a bed), eat well, and sleep a lot for three months. I remember sleeping a lot when we got home…waking up many times, with my husband sitting on the bed staring at me while I slept. He was wonderful in caring for me. He did everything in the house and for me.

We had planned an expensive honeymoon in the Mediterranean. We would lose deposits if we didn't go and I wanted to go anyway. In my spiritual beliefs and life, I felt I would be protected. I would simply take it easy. Everyone warned me about going so soon after the accident, but I have always had the philosophy that when your time is up, and you want to go, it is up; and if it isn't time for you, and you don't want to leave you won't go.

We wanted to experience another part of the world together. Bill had never been anywhere aside from a few places in the mainland, New Zealand, Canada and Hawaii. I wanted to give him the opportunity to experience and see other cultures and places, especially Italy and the United Kingdom (my cultural roots).

He, as an artist, would love to enjoy that art and civilization. The trip would broaden his experience and viewpoint; because up until this trip, he believed the best of everything, art, food, culture, history, etc. was Hawaiian. So we went, a few weeks after the accident, never telling my doctor, who had said rest for three months.

We flew to Barcelona Spain, arrived rested and began walking around. I had made a two night stay in the Castelldefels area, there, before embarking on the ship because of the 12 hours time difference. We were exactly 12 hours ahead of Molokai. We checked out after one night and drove to the pier for the cruise ship. Our ship? Not there. Wrong ship -- wrong day. We had to return to check back into the hotel. Things like that happened for a long while with my brain. I just couldn't think very well for a while. I guess it was just that my circulatory system just had to clear out all the blood on my cortex, and I had to rewire my thinking process for some things.

We noticed to our delight that Barcelona was full of lovers at all ages. A great many couples held hands there! Just like us! We had never seen that anywhere else in the world either of us had traveled. It was fun for us to watch other people walk along the very wide cement walkway along the beach and ocean holding hands like we do -- everywhere.

Our trip was extraordinary as we had expected. One of the more interesting things that Bill observed and brought back to tell his people in Molokai happened when we were in the Isle of Capri. Capri is a magnificent resort area with visitors from all over the world. They need, however, to import all of their drinking water, because they had pumped below a sustainable yield of potable water from their aquifer. Bill made sure to tell people upon our return that this must not happen on Molokai, for there was a very real threat of that on Molokai with the Molokai Ranch about to push for a large development.

—⚭—

Bill Kapuni started his Hawaiian Homestead Association, because he saw that Hawaiians needed to move forward together instead of remaining isolated in ohanas and separate neighborhood Island groups. Much like Kamaehameha I united the Islands under one sovereign, Bill thought there needed to be unity under one sovereign Hawaiian leadership for Hawaiian Homesteaders so that Hawaiians would have more political power over their own affairs.

He started an association called Kalamaula Mauka in the Aha pu'a o Molokai now called Mokupuni o Molokai.

He started the association so that it could be a member of the Sovereign Council of Hawaiian Homesteads Assembly (SCHHA), which is a statewide Hawaiian organization composed of Homesteaders throughout all Hawaii. I was appointed to its executive council by the chairman. This was a great honor as the first and only non-Hawaiian member. Some were skeptical of the color of my skin and wanted to have me taken off the council, but the Chairman valued me for my contributions and the Council recognized me as a Hawaiian at heart. The next chairman reappointed me and said at an executive council meeting, "I look at you and I see a Hawaiian".... (not just Hawaiian at heart)! I learned about the struggles native Hawaiians have historically had and continue to have in maintaining their culture and gaining their sovereignty.

Because of Bill's stature in the Hawaiian community, we were invited for two days and an overnight stay onto the USS Abraham Lincoln Aircraft Carrier during the Pacific war games with the Pacific Rim Alliance. The Navy was trying to create good public relations with Hawaiians because some of their sonar operations were under criticism. Hawaiians are environmentally sensitive people particularly when there is a possibility of interfering with sea life.

My accident was six weeks prior, and I let just one fleeting fearful moment in my mind about my neck and blood vessels in my brain, because the landing occurs when a hook from the plane is caught on a steel cable stretched across the deck of the carrier and the plane is stopped cold in three seconds! The opposite occurs when the plane takes off from the carrier. It is catapulted off the deck like being in a sling shot within a few seconds. I returned to my philosophy of life and decided to take advantage of experiencing this once in a lifetime opportunity. It was an extreme carnival ride!

As a civilian I was not wild about the military; having been a pacifist against wars earlier in my life. However, this experience of meeting the young people (18 years average) on this ship, and finding them personable, polite, dedicated, intelligent, knowledgeable and focused on their jobs shed new light on my old ideas; and as always in my life, I am grateful to learn and change.

Bill and I ready to take off for the USS Abraham Lincoln

PART III

CHAPTER THIRTY-ONE

About six months after we were married, I began to have dreams about a place, a beach, in Hawaii, I had never seen. It was a beautiful expansive white sand rocky beach that I was flying over and looking at from above. I had the dream two times and told Bill about it because of the importance of my dreams. I knew if there was a third, it would be very significant in our lives, but I did not know how.

In July, I had the third dream of the beach I had been seeing and finally recognized it on TV or in the paper. The beach was La'au Point located at the south west corner of the Island; and I told Bill we had to begin going to the meetings and learning what this was all about, because it was important to me in some way. Besides, Black Raven had taught me that when I was flying over something in my dreams, that the future had not yet been set and could be changed.

We attended our first meeting in July to learn about Molokai Ranch, an absent tee landlord in Singapore owning one third the Island, that wanted to develop 200 million dollar acre lots along the shoreline and through CC&Rs would place restrictions on beach access and keep fishing boats off the reef along the shoreline, which was the richest fishing and lobster hunting around the Island. I had served over three years on a planning commission on the mainland, and I knew a slick developer spiel when I heard one. These guys sounded the same, only more polished. They had definitely fooled a lot of the people on Island by the time Bill and I became involved.

Bill wasn't fooled. Early on he pulled out of the community meetings they were holding, because he saw through what they were doing; yet his name was included as one of the people who helped put the Ranch plan for developing La'au Point together. This was not the case. They had taken all the names of the participants from the sign in sheets at the meetings and made it seem like they were involved in setting up this plan--the Molokai Ranch Plan. In actuality the Ranch plan was already completed and the meetings were held simply to convince people developing La'au Point was a good thing to do for the Island.

The Middle of Molokai

I knew this beautiful Island of Molokai that I loved, even before Bill, was the last Hawaiian Island and needed to be protected from further subdivision development and intrusion by outside cultures that would change and influence the native Hawaiian culture here even more then it already had. I knew that this Island population depended upon the ocean and the land for their subsistence. 37% of the people on Molokai lived subsistence living off the aina and ocean. Here in Molokai, still yet, Hawaiians are not crowded out by new cultures and prevented from practicing their traditional ways of living. I am grateful that this Island provides for Hawaiians the opportunity to live from the ocean and off the land as they have traditionally done over eons of time.

A friend asked me once why I worked so hard to save this Island. My answer was simple: my husband lived subsistence living a good bit of his life and might not have been around for me here and now if he had not learned subsistence living from his Tutu in Oahu and been able to have a place to practice it in Molokai.

Bill didn't know I was a long time environmentalist and quasi activist, who worked on the inside as a lobbyist or commissioner, (not activist on the outside) but an environmentalist never the less. I had seen many times how developers touched the earth and it became sore. After many planning meetings held by activist leaders and attended by Bill and I, and others, I focused on the law protecting Hawaiian land from development if it has been continuously used by Hawaiians for traditional culture and religious ceremonies.

Bill and I weighed in against the La'au Point development and opinion started to shift. The battle was on. Native Hawaiians are permitted anywhere in Hawaii to have beach access from the ocean fifty feet into the shoreline. It was decided to build a Hale (house) on the 50 feet access shoreline at La'au Point.

Some of the activists cut and trimmed mango trees from the east end of the Island and loaded them onto the trailer Bill attached to his four wheel drive diesel truck. We brought them to Kaunakakai to our house overnight. We were going to have to transport the mango logs to the west end in a caravan for safety, because we had to traverse through Ranch Land to reach Hale O Lono (house of the shark) Harbor where we would move the logs to boats. This was going to be a big job and none of us knew if we would have any help when we arrived at the harbor. We knew of only one boat and two people that would be waiting for us.

Early the next morning as we descended the hill over a long dirt road to the Harbor through the Ranch lands, I saw an owl fly across our path and knew it was a good sign. I told everyone change was coming.

When we approached the harbor, we all breathed a sigh of relief, for the warriors had come! There were many young men waiting for the logs to arrive. In silent unison the young men began the heavy work of moving the long tree logs from the trailer to the four boats that had come. They worked as a team instinctively knowing what to do. Bill was physically unable; so being fairly strong, I mistakenly attempted to assist, and was politely told it was for the men to do it alone.

We brought the logs by truck as far as we could. We had to use the boats from there to get the logs to La'au Point, because there were no roads and the remaining land to the point was all Ranch lands. I watched as one boat came alongside the loading dock, was loaded, and took off down the shoreline to La'au Point. Then another boat came up for a load and then another and another. There were four boats that had come, and they continued the trip down and back until everything had been moved to the Point. Word was out and everyone contributed what they had whether it be boats, food, water, muscle or aloha.

The leader and his wife, Bill and I took the last boat with the water and food. We arrived at the beach chosen for the Hale. It was breathtaking…a carved out area in the land large enough for a small harbor. The water was too rough to land the boats, so the warriors swam out to the boats and unloaded the logs one by one. Then they guided and carried the logs on their shoulders to shore all the while treading water! It was an unbelievable scene watching all the Hawaiian warriors in the water with the waves crashing over their heads and the logs.

They were very tired I could tell by the way they were heavily breathing in the water when they came to our boat to get the food and drinking water. Actually, they lost some of the water which was the only thing they did not get to shore. They saw the water jugs through the crystal clear light blue/green water they had been swimming in and eventually did retrieve them when the ocean was tamer. But, not that day, they were too tired.

The leader and his wife jumped into the water and asked me to come with them ashore. I wanted to go. I could see all the people gathered on shore. There would be prayers, chants and ceremonies, and I wanted to be a part of it. I looked at Bill. He was unable to go. He was too weak to get into the water and tread or swim. I looked at him again. He looked down, and I turned and said to them I would stay with Bill.

Bill and I watched from the boat someone striking into the ground, the flag pole with the Hawaiian flag proudly flying, and the people forming a large circle to hold hands and have ceremony; although we could not hear them with the wind blowing and the boat too far away on the ocean, we watched this momentous occasion. The Molokai warriors were taking a stand against the Ranch. They had taken a beach hold for their culture....for their spirituality.... for their ancestors, who were buried in these sandy beaches, and for their traditional Hawaiian lifestyle. We were proud to have contributed and be a part of it.

—⁓—

Every year there is an outrigger canoe race from Molokai to Oahu. Every year Bill would attend the canoe races to see all his old buddies from his canoe racing days. He won the koa race division one year when he was only eighteen. Without missing a stroke in the synchronized paddling, never breaking their rhythm each paddler would change up several times during a race so that an alternate could take over and give him a rest in the escort boat. During a change up, the paddler would jump into the water as the alternate would jump in the canoe from the other side and begin paddling. When they finished this six hour race, Bill did not even know they had won, and his team mates had to carry him out of the canoe, because he had had only two takeouts during the six hours and his legs were cramped and he couldn't move them.

The race was a lot different now than when he raced. He slept in army pup tents on the beach before his races, and now the paddlers stay in hotel rooms or with friends and family before the race. Now there are 100 canoes from around the world. Then it was just neighbor Island paddlers participating with around 12 canoes.

Bill and I had decorated his truck with anti La'au development signs several of the wahine leaders had made for the yards of sympathizers to the fight. He built a one by two inch wooden frame to be fastened on his truck, and together we decided what hand painted and decorated signs would be nailed where on the frame. To top it all off he took out his Hawaiian flag which had been used in many environmental wars before like the Cruise ship and a subdivision east end in the 80's and flew it from the truck proudly.

Bill's truck with homemade
anti-development signs and Hawaiian flag

We were going to take the truck with all its' decoration and the granddaughters and our girls (two German Shepard mixes Loke and Hoku we got as puppies) down to Hale O Lono for the canoe races to Oahu. The night before, all six of us slept at Dixie Maru beach, where a protest march to Laau Point was to start early at sun rise.

We awoke at dawn to the sound of people gathering for the march. The crowd grew and grew. The day before the Ranch Manager had asked Bill what the Ranch should do with the People walking through ranch lands. Bill said "Let them go through." The Ranch took Bill's advice for Bill knew how volatile Hawaiian warriors could be. The Ranch even provided water at points on the shoreline.

After all the marchers left Dixie Maru walking on the trail, including an 80 year old Kapuna, all wearing T-shirts with A'ole La'au, which means Stop La'au across the back, and the words, Keep Molokai Molokai, on the front; we got in the truck to go to the canoe race where the crews were making ready checking their rigging on the canoes and covering them. Seeing our signs and speaking with Bill (even filming him in an interview), many people said they were sympathetic to the fight we were in, but shook their heads saying we couldn't win against the developer. Nobody ever does.

That evening Bill was able to tell the Navigator of the Hokulea when Eddie drowned going for help after the voyaging canoe had capsized, why he had never joined voyaging canoe trips. Bill had promised Eddie's father that he would not paddle on a voyaging canoe, because 'Pop' asked him not to after he had already lost one son to the ocean, and couldn't loose another. (Bill was the hanai son and part of the Aikau family.)

During High School at Farrington, he lived with the Aikau family, and Bill and Eddie were inseparable...cutting classes when the "surf was up." They life-guarded together saving many lives. Bill was one that Eddie saved; when Bill, while surfing, called a wave he shouldn't have, and it turned him off his board sending him down to the bottom. Eddie was with him and saw Bill's board come up. Knowing Bill was in a life and death struggle with Kanaloa ocean water, Eddie dove under and miraculously brought Bill to the surface. Bill always felt he owed Eddie his life.

In a return visit to Hawaii after Bill moved to Washington State, he brought some friends (16 girls) from the mainland for the luau Eddie put on for celebrating Bill's return home to Hawaii. As Bill told it, he introduced Eddie to his wife to be, and they took off together and he never saw Eddie again during his visit home.

—〰—

This is what the Navigator of the Hokulea voyaging canoe had never understood about Bill…why he never paddled a voyaging canoe? It is an important status among Hawaiians to paddle in voyaging canoes. His absence was noticeable. Bill was a natural athlete and a Hawaiian water man. He had been a champion paddler, knew the ocean, and was spiritually connected to Kanaloa. As I watched the two men talk, I knew Bill was relieved that this man finally knew why he had been absent from the voyages.

We awoke at dawn to see the canoes off. It was a colorful exciting sight as we watched the canoes dash to the ocean from the beach with their escort boats following. This was a wonderful time for us with the granddaughters. We had all been together laughing and helping the cause to save Molokai from development at La'au point.

CHAPTER THIRTY-TWO

BILL HAD BEEN TO SEE DOCTORS that fall because he was not feeling very well. The culprit was Plavix which had been prescribed for him two years earlier even when he had not had a heart attach or stroke. Plavix causes internal bleeding and it did that to Bill. He went to the hospital in December that year before Christmas with only five and half units of blood in his massive body. Anyone else would have died. A man his size would normally have 12 or 13 units and losing over half your blood is a sure sign you're not going to make it.

Once we were at the Honolulu Hospital and learned Bill would need an operation, I asked to be in the operating room to help him. Before answering, he asked me, "Who is this guy?" He's not just a wood carver is he?" I told him, 'no' and explained a little about us and our healing. He persisted with his questions, and I finally told him Bill was a Kahuna. He then immediately agreed I could be with Bill during the operation. I held onto his feet during the procedure grounding him here in space, time and place also.

Hospitals are not good places for traditional Hawaiians who are from and live in the culture. It certainly was not a good place for my husband and as soon as the surgeon said we could leave we wanted to get out. Bill's heart doctor had other plans.

I felt like he was being used as a guinea pig to experiment on. Because almost every tort case involves medical injury, I learned a good deal involving the medical profession. I knew how to read test results and doctors and nurses notes and reports. I knew from one test I had seen so far in Molokai General that my husband's blood tests were like a final exam for an advanced degree in medicine. I knew what caused elevations from the norm in blood tests. If a doctor started 'messing around with his blood' it would go up and down for a long time because of the intricacies in the blood chemistry and the effects food and medicine had on the blood.

I was 'blown away" by the fact that my husband was in the hospital at all, that his blood tests were so complicated, and blown away by this heart doctor; who, although the other surgeon who operated on him for the condition on which he was admitted to the hospital had released him, put her arm around him and said (while looking at me) "He's staying with me. I'm not releasing him from the hospital".

I was sent out of his room to sleep that night, and I was no longer able to sleep on the ward in a vacant room that had couches stored in it, because it was 'a liability for the hospital and too dangerous'. After tossing and turning for a few hours, in the elevator lobby on a loveseat couch, I returned to his room and asked him what he wanted to do. He was awake also and said, "Leave". I said, "OK". We prayed and I slept in his bed with him those last few hours that night, because our energies were being stripped by all that we felt in the hospital and that room particularly. We were stronger together. There was no peace and quiet with the constant interruptions of the nurses and general noise on the floor.

When the first morning nurse came in, I said no more tests, we are leaving; and then I asked for a copy of all his medical records from this stay. I received them. The doctor called him on the cell phone and said, "if you leave I'm not going to be your doctor any more." He said, "fine, you are not my doctor any more". We left the hospital together. He was walking and we got home fine. She had refused to give him any medications when he left without her authorization; but later apparently,

changed her mind because the Molokai pharmacy said they had prescriptions for him.

He rested and I took good care of him through Christmas and into the New Year. With Bill's 60th birthday and our anniversary in January, he still yet remembered me with flowers. He even went out and got them for me! Bill was always romantic.

CHAPTER THIRTY-THREE

THE DEVELOPERS HAD SUBMITTED THEIR EIS (Environmental Impact Statement) on the proposed Laau Point development. We had to write and submit by a certain postmark date questions within four weeks. Bill was still recuperating and laying in the lazy boy a lot in the living room next to the word processor. He remained there all the time praying for me while I attempted this monumental task in four weeks with my dyslexia; and now, in addition, my dysfunctional brain activity from the accident, that still gave me big surprise memory lapses quite often.

I described my brain as being like that black eight ball toy when you turned it upside down and asked it questions, it would take a while before an answer would surface to be read. That is what it was like for me. Some parts of my memory were good, others ok, others were gone for hours, days maybe longer. I couldn't add and subtract numbers with accuracy. I knew I forgot things for months at a time. I began trying to write things down that would come up in my 8 ball brain that I had forgotten, but often I couldn't remember to write them down fast enough.

I had been out of the practice of law for about twelve or thirteen years and not accustomed to this type of intense brain focus activity anymore in my retirement. I was at a place in my life where I was having fun for once…retired! But I knew I had to do this, no one else on Island could do what I was capable of. I struggled and forced myself because of the monumental importance my questions might have on the outcome.

It was all meant to be this way for I felt passionately about stopping the La'au development and the passion motivated me to stay on it. By forcing myself to work my brain in this type of activity, I was exercising it and learning new ways of getting around the damaged synapses like what my son had done years before. My fighting for the underdog personality and revulsion of tearing up sacred Hawaiian land for a wealthy subdivision to make money while unearthing ancestor graves, and my dreams of La'au Point, all motivated me to keep trying.

I had attended the first Land Use Commission initiation meeting where we were told the Commission had NEVER turned down a housing subdivision, and the only way they might was if the developer mislead or lied in the EIS. I knew what I had to do now. I just had to find a way to do it.

I prayed a lot and finally made a breakthrough on the water issues and after six times reading the water sections, which were buried in many places throughout the EIS, finally figured out how they were masking facts and misleading the water resource availability the Ranch's anticipated use pre and post their proposed development of La'au Point.

I placed my discoveries on a table so that it was perfectly clear for all to understand and respond to. I cited pages from their reports where I found the facts throughout the 250+ page document to support my table. They did not respond to it. As a matter of fact, they completely avoided it and didn't even put my questions about water or my table in their EIS answers! Counting the sub-parts to all the questions, there were about 1500 questions I was able to ask.

We celebrated after I was finished, because Bill likewise was feeling much better having rested those weeks while I was working. We went through the spring happy, although his daughter got pregnant instead of having counseling. Bill was very concerned. We had been asked by friends to raise her two daughters, because people thought she and her husband were not giving them enough stability. With him becoming physically weakened, he now had to worry about a third Grandbaby he would be unable to protect. His illness was taking control of his life about one half the time now. Both those issues would pull us down from spirit; and we would have to work ourselves back up with prayer and meditation. We prayed a lot now.

Bill was only able to be active about half the time now so he solicited help from his son-in-law. He had apprenticed him, a Mexican young man who had been an illegal alien to America. He made it to Hawaii by boat and lived at the Molokai Shores Hotel across the street from Bill's house. He met and married Bill's daughter, and Bill took him under his wing. He helped him get a green card and tried to teach him how to carve in the ways of Hawaiian protocol and traditions. Bill asked for help from him as the Maui Festival of Canoes was fast approaching, but he refused to assist and help him. Bill needed assistance in cutting, bringing home the tree stump, cutting the stumps out, but no help was forth coming from his 'family'. He worked at his own pace as best he could.

His son-in-law was a Mexican and not Hawaiian. He did not understand Hawaiian protocol and traditions. His daughter should have known to have him help and assist her father. But she did not!

CHAPTER THIRTY-FOUR

IT WAS PAINFUL TO WATCH THIS once strong invincible, energetic husband weaken before my eyes. I wasn't able to process the decline, because for me his Spirit was still strong, and we lived in spirit with not much ado about the physical world. Sunday, on Mother's Day, he wasn't feeling well so he called his daughter up at 9:00 AM asking her to bring the granddaughters, who always brought joy to him, down for a visit. She said she would. He moved himself to a chair out on the porch and sat there three hours in that chair waiting for her to come. She didn't call to let him know she was not coming. She just made him wait. At noon he went into the bed and laid down. He woke up after six and could barely walk. I called the ambulance and we found ourselves in the Honolulu Hospital again. This time it was a cellulites infection in his legs and blood loss again.

Shortly after our arrival in his room, a cot was brought in the room for me to sleep on…no more couches by the elevator. I never left him. The infection left by Wednesday and he was ready to leave; but not having been moved, except for a sponge bath only once, his muscles had atrophied and he couldn't move. Leaving a 20 year old motionless for four days would cause atrophy let alone a 60 years old. He could talk, but he couldn't move.

This was devastating to him. He was an athlete who prided himself on his athleticism and physical strength his whole life and now he couldn't even move at all? Thursday, his brother came in and with Tough Love talk motivated him into moving a little. I got him to sit up and fed him a little. He seemed happy that he could do that much, but he was very depressed Friday. After hearing he might not walk again, he stopped eating entirely. Although all the numbers in his blood tests improved, he became more depressed and didn't move, didn't eat and withdrew more and more. I saw him sinking further and further into his bed. He had withdrawn so much by now I was crying to myself because I knew he was dying. He was dying. He had given up.

The liaison nurse, who knew the medical side of healing and our spiritual side of healing with energy work, and had requested the Healing Touch energy worker, came in when I was breaking. I finally broke that morning and cried and cried. She asked me what was wrong and I said "He's dying. He'll be dead in a week if I don't get him out of here and home." She asked me if I couldn't "hold him up in my energy any more?" I said, "I can't. I have very little energy left to give", I responded. She asked, "Can't you go outside and replenish?" I responded, "No, not here in the city". Not when I am on empty in this Hospital.

We had started using the Healing Touch people in the hospital by Wednesday (the fourth day) thanks to this liaison nurse and his main doctor who also understood and accepted the need of different healing approaches and practices in getting him well. The sessions helped us both the first time and he went into spirit and I was relieved. Thursday, it did not pull him up very much. He not only was not eating, moving, talking, but he was not even opening his eyes. He wanted to go home but was not able to move. On Thursday, I had stopped all tests and said we were leaving on Sunday. That was the soonest I was able to make the plane reservations and I worked backward from that point. The doctors responded angrily and started ordering all kinds of tests which I stopped.

The lead doctor was the one I had the most rapport with and she had ordered only one test. I then called her cell as to why and she explained that although the infection was gone, his white blood cell count was elevating and she wanted to know why and wanted a cat scan of his organs. I asked for a copy of all his records and she saw to it that I got them. After reading the test results and understanding her position, and feeling the energy of his organs and knowing there was no infection there; I felt confident when I called her back in making an agreement with her that she could do the Cat scan of his organs; but if she found nothing there, she would let us go home. That was all right with me as I remembered the test result which concerned her. She agreed but said she couldn't count on what the other doctors would say. We went through that procedure. It was negative as I had said it would be.

Then I had two more doctors and the nurses to work on just for some positive energy to be around us. Thursday night, the kidney doctor ordered another test which I stopped, because after questioning her, she admitted she could get the same information from the blood tests.

Then at 11:00 pm a nurse came in with a shot class of a silver glistening metallic looking liquid. I asked what that was. He gave me the name. I said what does it do and what was it ordered for? He explained it was for contrast in a cat scan tomorrow. I said there would be no more scans, he already had the one today; and no more tests would be performed on him.

We were leaving Sunday. I made them take out the shot glass and the urine testing paraphernalia in the bathroom. There would be no more tests on my husband! He was going to leave Sunday. After I did this, the head nurse from the floor out of the blue came in and said "I'm glad you did that Mrs. Kapuni, if he had drank that it would have ripped out what kidneys he has left."

I sort of slept some that night, but wondered what would happen next. Friday was calm. No one came to see him, but the lead doctor. I thanked her for bringing in the Healing Touch people for us. She asked me a little about how my husband and I healed. I said do you know about the Tibetan monks moving out of their bodies? She said she did. I said my husband and I usually live in spirit -- about one to three feet off the ground. "Do you see this cement floor?" as I touched the floor with my hand. "Well my husband and I are usually here", as I lifted my hand up in the air, "walking up here when we are happy and in spirit" when you live in a spiritual reality, there is no disease. We pray a great deal to stay in that place of no time and space. I think she understood a little.

We believed sickness or disease is just that.... a dis ease about your person that brings about a non-harmonious function in one or more of your body system(s) inside your body. If you are with God in spirit, you can not be at dis ease....all is harmonious in Spirit. There had to be a reason this man could come into the hospital two times with only about five plus pints of blood in his body and not die and be able to leave once walking and this time maybe by wheel chair. He lived in Spirit.

I spoke to the social worker to get assistance to leave. There was no assistance on Sunday. I called the van services in town and found only one open on Sundays, and he was able to come at the time I needed him in order to catch the plane without too much time for Bill to be in the chair traveling and getting tired. Island Air said they would take care of him if I could get him to the gate. They would take him up to and down from the plane in the wheelchair and move him in and out of the seat once in the airplane. All I had to do was get him to the gate. That's all.

I would have to work on the other end getting assistance once I was at the Molokai airport, because his daughter told people I was taking him out of the hospital without doctor's authorization, so the people I had lined up to help move him home did not want to help now. I was just going to have to continue to follow spiritual guidance and everything would then work the way it was supposed to. Now I needed a wheelchair and walker for the trip home. I found only one place that was open on Saturday and called his brother to take me there in the morning. Bill kept asking me if we were leaving and when are we going home? I just kept telling him what I was doing to get him out of there.

CHAPTER THIRTY-FIVE

I SLEPT VERY LITTLE FRIDAY NIGHT worrying about all that had to be done and the biggest -- how was I going to get Bill up and in the wheelchair when he was paralyzed? I just kept praying. I was trying to trust and follow spirit fighting for my husband's life as I moved through the negative energy I was facing. He was leaving this world and I wasn't ready to let him go. He had pulled back so much. He hadn't eaten since Thursday when his brother was visiting. He didn't even open his eyes anymore. The only sign of life he ever had in his eyes from Thursday night on was when I talked about going home; then he would open his eyes. That was the hope he was clinging to. The western hospitals, for the most part, ignore the spiritual part of a human being, let alone a traditional Hawaiian; and they simply deal with and try and heal the physical body.

My husband needed to be outside to see the sky and feel the breezes and spirits, see the aina, the trees, the leaves blowing with makani, to smell the earth and inhale the energy all around him. He needed to be with the natural world that had been him, been his life, been his source of creativity and sustenance. He was part of nature as we all are, but for Bill, it was more so, because he was more so. He lived most of his life, particularly now, in spirit and connected to the ocean, land and the forces of nature. As a medical person agreed, he lives in spirit. "No one can live in the material world with only five pints of blood in their body."

After speaking with ombudsmen and nurses who had aligned with us getting out, I learned that if I could get him in a wheel chair, there was nothing the hospital could do about our leaving. That then became my goal and I knew, of course, they would not help me at all, because they didn't want him to leave. It was just Bill and me fighting everyone else.

The next morning I knew something was going to happen, I could feel it. I wondered what. His brother came to take me to rent the equipment I needed to take Bill home. As we were walking out, who should appear but Bill's daughter. I took her into his room and she was horrified and started to cry. "This is not my father." I replied, "This is not the man I married either." I left them together staying focused and determined to complete my essentials so that we could leave the next day.

Upon my return, his daughter had placed her backpack on my bed and plugged in her cell phone by my bed. I thought that was a bad sign. It was. She wanted to take my place and stay with him at the hospital! She had no idea of the statistics for staying in the hospital. The longer you stay the more likely you are to become more sick with something else. He had already been in there one week total this time. I said no. That was the end of that. She said she wanted him to stay in the hospital; and I said it was not her decision, she was only the daughter, I was the wife, and Bill wanted to go home, and that was that.

I discovered while I was gone the doctors and his daughter had tried to get him to say he wanted to stay in the hospital. He didn't. He told them to ask me, his wife. Bill was extremely vulnerable more so then ever in his life, because he was paralyzed and his physical strength and power were always his protection before. He had very little strength and mana left at that point. It was his most vulnerable time in his life. But he held his ground before three doctors and his daughter! Four of them around his bed when he was paralyzed! He simply referred them to me.

I had been fighting everyone to get him out and keep him stable and ready for the trip home. I had been with him 24/7 for seven days in the hospital and could hardly take any more stress. I knew what my husband wanted and needed. They all wanted him to go on dialysis which was never an option for Bill. He had very small veins and had an uncle on dialysis and things didn't work out for him. Besides, the bigger issue was he was Hawaiian and he was not going to be on a machine....not tied to a machine and never go into the ocean again. That was it. He had spoken. He never wavered on that issue....not once. The answer was always the same – even when I asked him once. It was his choice not anyone else's! Lots of people chose to die rather then go on dialysis. Why couldn't people accept Bill Kapuni had wishes for himself that needed to be respected and honored? Only his brother agreed with me that it was his call and everyone needed to respect that and back off.

Things were quiet and I was wondering when the next shoe would drop. It did. His daughter came back with who she said was family. I said "how come I have never met you if you are family?" The silence was telling, but I was not expecting who she turned out to be. They asked if they could be alone with him and I asked Bill. He said it was OK and after all, it was his adopted daughter. I said they could have a half hour and then I was going to close up the room for the night because tomorrow was the big day.

I went down stairs for my dinner, but was only gone ten minutes when I felt him calling me back so I returned to the room. They had closed the door and were trying to get him to say they could all talk to the doctors with him together, and that he could go home with her...this new family girl in the room. This was the second "invitation" he had had to go home with someone other than his wife. His daughter had asked him that earlier in the day as if they had forgotten Bill was my husband and we were married? Why were all these people coming out of the woodwork all of a sudden?

This drama and craziness was almost more then I could take at this point. They were crowding and leaning over him. His daughter was at his feet rubbing his legs and feet. He told me later he "didn't like her energy at all. Something was wrong with it." I heard this girl, I didn't know, say two times while I was there in the room that if he "left the hospital, he would die within three days"! The second time she made her unbelievably negative statement, he replied, "So be it. I want to die in Molokai in my own bed". After which, I said, "OK the room is closing for the night now. I'm asking you to leave now." The unknown 'family' member leaned over and kissed him and said she wanted his dolphin carving! What crazy making! It was too much craziness for me.

I was stressed to the max, and to have all this craziness occur before the big day (Sunday) that no one believed was going to happen was almost too much for me to bear, and I broke down again with just Bill and I in the room alone after the two girls left. Bill was upset that this girl had kissed him and he couldn't do anything about it. "She couldn't have done that if I could move," he said. I comforted him.

He said to me, "are we leaving"? I said, "Yes". He said, "They all think you are wrong to take me out of here don't they"? I said, "Yes". He said, "I have to get out then and prove them wrong". All things happen for a reason. I was glad their visit angered him enough to motivate him to get up and leave tomorrow. Anger is a valuable motivator sometimes. He told me that night, "You have to get me up, and dressed early while I have the strength. I will lose energy if I am not up in the chair by 10." I said, "OK" and nodded my head.

CHAPTER THIRTY-SIX

W E WOKE EARLY SUNDAY. I GOT his shirt and shorts on, and jacked the bed up so he was half way sitting up. All three doctors came in. The lead doctor first and asked him if he was going home and he said, "Yes". She asked him "how" and he said, "By plane". We all three smiled at his humor. She smiled because she knew he couldn't move, and we wouldn't be going anywhere. She said, "Can you get out of the bed"? He said, "Yes". She asked him to show her and he declined. She smiled and left the room knowing we wouldn't be leaving.

The infection doctor came in next and was still worried about the elevated white blood cell count. I acknowledged his concern. The Kidney doctor came in last and I said, "Look at his face. He is happy to be going home". She acknowledged that much. I held no animosity towards the doctors or nurses. They were only medically trained, and they were just trying to do what they thought was best for my husband. They thought it was best for him to be on a kidney machine. Never mind what he wanted. Isn't that what everyone tries to do, their best? They did not understand us, our spiritual world or what is beyond the physical body. They only knew their medical remedies not spiritual ones. She was trying to force him on a kidney machine, because she thought that was what was best for him. She was not taking into consideration what he wanted. Besides they all knew we were not going to be able to leave because my husband was paralyzed. They all left the room with a smile.

Everyone left, but there were still several nurses there watching in the doorway. I told them to leave. One said she had to stay because it was hospital policy. I jacked up the upper part of the bed so that it put his back as upright as possible. I then moved to the side behind him and pushed him forward with all my might and stuffed a pillow behind his back. I was jacking him up like a car jack raises a car. I did this three or four times, each time placing another pillow behind his back until he was sitting upright.

Then I had to move his very heavy legs each weighing at least 70 pounds around to the side of the bed; and, eventually, moving each leg little by little, so as not to twist him too much, and got both feet on the ground. I then jacked up the elevation of the bed itself so that his long legs were almost straight with his feet being flat on the floor.

Next I got the walker they had jerry rigged with extenders on the hand holds so that he had a crutch to place under each arm. I then had to straighten him out and move the wheel chair closer to him alongside the bed and facing him. My idea was to get him standing and then somehow swing him 90 degrees into the wheelchair. I placed the breaks on the chair so it wouldn't move if he went flying into it fast.

I looked at the clock and knew he wanted to be in the chair by 10, and the van was coming at 11. It was 9:40 now. Now came the part we were going to need God, angels, spirits everyone we could call upon to help get him from this position of leaning forward with his butt against the bed to get him into a standing position and then turned ninety degrees to sit in the wheelchair. He had no grip or strength in his hands…only the crutches to lean on under his arms. He had no mobile power at all.

We prayed and I called his Tutu, my Tutu, everyone I knew, all his spirits and, of course God to help us. We prayed and I stood in front of him with my head on his head. Crown chakra to crown chakra and I recited the vision of his legs being koa trees that were going to hold him up while he stood and turned into the chair. We tried a few times unsuccessfully.

I kept praying and saying the vision and asking for help over and over again. Over and over again. He finally was able to stand up leaning a little forward on the crutches with our heads still together to balance and support him physically, mentally and spiritually. Then I worked on getting him to move his left leg toward the chair and turning towards me. All the while I am holding him up to keep him steady, with one foot braced against the walker so that it would not move, and the other foot back (leg bent) bracing our joint weight from him falling forward. He tried once and then again and then again. I told him to make the directions in his head go through his body and down to his legs through the channels. (Similar visions I made for my son 20 years earlier when he was in the hospital.)

Then, he moved his left leg towards the chair and then the right leg and then fell into the chair as he moved his left leg again. The nurse at the doorway yelled, "He's in!" The next nurse down the hall yelled 'he's in' and it went down the hall to the nurses' station where the doctors were. Now the doctors had to scurry to get all the meds filled by the pharmacy down stairs. They never thought we would do it! Those three steps took us 40 minutes!

I have to say I was sweating when Bill fell back into the chair. I may also have been sweating from the energy of all the light moving through my body. (When I work on someone, so much energy goes through my body, I sweat most times.) I never gave up. Never believed for an instant we were not going home that day. I packed up my things and prepared to take him out. He was anxious to leave. His daughter came in and asked if she could talk to him privately. He said, "Anything you have to say to me can be said in front of my wife. Stand by me Victoria". With that I came and stood next to him and she turned and left. Why wouldn't she help or at least talk to him, especially if she thought he was going to die in three days?

He wanted to get out of the room so I wheeled him down the hall. Many of the nurses lined the hall and a few smiled. I took him to the nurse's station and parked him while I went back to the room to get the things I had brought and the few things he accumulated from the hospital that we would need at home. I came back and they were hurrying their medication requests from pharmacy and his paperwork. No one was prepared for us to leave. No one but Bill and I believed we would be leaving.

It was almost time for the van to be outside and I loaded what I could on the wheelchair and in his lap and proceeded to the elevator. His adopted daughter and 'her member of the family' (who ended up being the daughter of Bill's ex-girlfriend!) were at the elevators. The so called family girl looked at me, squinted her eyes with hate and said "I'll see you in Molokai at his funeral." I was so surprised anyone would say anything like that to someone leaving the hospital all I could say was "Why don't you turn your negativity into a positive and turn to God for prayer? That would be more helpful. Pray for him." With that we turned to the elevators and left.

As soon as we were outside, I watched him perk up. He lifted his head and opened his eyes bigger to see the leaves on the trees, the green grass, and looked around at the clouds and sky. His mood had already changed! I was right. He started coming alive. He felt the wind and sun and saw the palm trees sway. Then I knew I had done the right thing! Not until that moment did I know 100% for sure. I had just been following divine guidance. My heart was singing as I watched him come alive. I had just been trying to stay in light with God and following what I was being directed to do, and knowing that my husband had been dying in the hospital and knowing if he did not leave, he would surely have died. If he was out, he would live. He needed to be connected to Nature. He was Hawaiian.

The hardest part of the day was over. I had gotten him (with the help of God and angels and guides and others) out of the hospital. He was complaining that he needed sunglasses, so the driver pulled up to K Mart for me to fly in and purchase a pair. He was going to be OK. Before Bill and I married he told me very sternly, "to marry me, you'll have to be a warrior and stand by me, and I will be your warrior and stand by you." I believe I did just that, and he did that for me and continues to do that for me to this day. The elevated white blood count, was most likely caused by a badly decayed and infected tooth that had to be pulled a few weeks later when he was ambulatory.

CHAPTER THIRTY SEVEN

I STILL NEEDED TO GET HIM home to Molokai and up those twelve steps into the house and then somehow get him walking and moving again. We arrived at Ho'olehua airport and Island Air took him off the plane. There I was with my husband, 340 lbs in a wheel chair unable to move. I pushed him towards the curb and there appeared an angel, who said she would take him home. We tried with some of the TSA employees to get him into her RV but couldn't. She left to get her pickup truck and came back, and Airport Security got him into the pick up bed lying down with his head propped up on something in the truck. We stopped at the Mormon Church on the way home. She gathered some of the men at church to come and help. I had to be taken to the hospital to pickup my car still there yet, and more importantly, to get from its' trunk the EMT's fabric stretcher so that Bill could be lifted up the stairs to our house.

We all arrived at the house, and I was so grateful for all the assistance -- Molokai people, their love of Bill Kapuni and the Island spirit supporting people in times of need is incredible. They placed him in the recliner where he could sit and sleep comfortably.

I needed to leave at 3:45pm to pick up my friend from the airport. She had traveled from Laramie, Wyoming, to be with us for the Festival of Canoes in Lahina this week. She would be a help for me to care for my husband. She was 81 years old and would not be able to move him, but she could give me emotional support; for I could not break now when he was home and totally my responsibility.

I promised the doctors I would bring him in for a checkup Wednesday and had no way to get him to the out patient clinic. I called on my friends from the La'au Point fight. They came and lifted him up into his wheelchair, down the 12 steps into the back of their pickup, up the steps to the outpatient clinic to discover the doctor didn't make it over from Oahu that day.

Bill was out of the house and in a truck so the boys then decided to take him for a ride through town and more importantly to the harbor where he had spent so much of his life near the water and boats. All of it definitely perked him up. The harbor always made him happy. We would drive there quite often just for him to 'see what was going on'.

Even though he was slumped over from the paralysis in his wheel chair going through town, and people thought he had had a stroke, he was revived by his outing. He came home and asked me to dial the Canoe Festival to speak with the Director and hold the phone for him, because he had no grip in his hands or movement in his arms. I did, he made arrangements with her for attending the parade and closing ceremony! I looked at him surprised when I hung up the phone for him. He was determined and energized to make the festival.

I knew if I was able to get him there, he would make a quantum leap again because all those people at the festival in Maui loved him so much and would lift him up with prayers and aloha. I just had to figure out how to get him there and keep holding him in my energy. I had to look into getting assistance. I got a local warrior to be his escort to help move him and take care of him with my friend and me once we were there.

We had been able to get a hospital bed in the living room for him and I began the job of caring for a totally paralyzed husband myself. We could not afford to pay for assistance or therapy. I just had to do it alone with him. He had a massive athletic body that just needed to be brought back from the brink. Part of the therapy was going to Maui, because I knew the aloha of the people in Maui for him would lift him in spirit.

Friday morning, (just four days out of the hospital) the day of the trip to Maui, while I got him bathed and dressed, he actually moved his arms when sitting in bed. He had been practicing and not told me. He flashed me that big smile of his when he showed me.

He was indeed proud of himself! Three men from our church would somehow get him into a vehicle and get him to and on the ferry. Bill's adopted daughter, ex-girlfriend and two granddaughters were on the same ferry and passed by us without saying one word to him! This was one of three times I watched his heart crack by actions and words, in this case NO words of caring, comfort, or concern, from his adopted daughter and his two grand daughters toward him. I simply didn't understand her hate and non-caring behavior at all. She appeared so cold and callous lacking compassion and love towards her father. She was pregnant, and typically during pregnancy, women are more compassionate and loving.

When we arrived, the Executive Director was obviously taken aback to see how incapacitated Bill was but took it in stride. It didn't bother me, because I had seen such a change from his dying in the hospital bed, to outside the hospital, to home, to watching him seeing my friend arrive, to going to the doctor and seeing the harbor, to making the decision to go to the festival, to getting on the ferry, I knew he would just keep on improving throughout the weekend. We needed a great deal of assistance getting him in and out of vehicles/ wheelchair from men in his hui on Maui at the festival and security at the hotel. During the weekend we, and others, were amazed at how he improved. He was able to stand holding onto the car door by the end of the weekend!

Saturday morning, the day of the parade, came and Bill was sitting on the bed doing calisthenics with his arms he was so excited! We laughed. We went to eat breakfast, when I received a return call from the sponsor I had called earlier that morning about arrangements for Bill to be on the float. She said they did not want Bill to go on the float because of liability. His heart sank and he said we'd go to Hana instead of the parade then.

I immediately went to meet with the three managers in charge and to look at the float. He could get on it and be stable with the wheelchair breaks and our strong Molokai warrior would be standing by him making sure the chair would not move. One of the managers was Hawaiian, and realized if Bill was not in the parade there would be pilikia surrounding the drum. We all understood, and shortly they called back and said he could come on the float. Hearing the news, he was happy and flashed that smile of his. There would not even be any difficulty getting him and his chair on the float because the back of the truck had a lift on it. As soon as he got on the float, it changed him again. He was smiling now with honor and pride on the float as his warrior held an umbrella over him for shade.

That evening when I accepted the Pahu carver's award for my husband, I thanked everyone for their prayers and aloha. They, the people with their prayers and aloha, lifted him up; and I was so grateful to them for their loving spirit. From that day on, everyday he got stronger and happier and was, once again, looking forward to a future. It was all meant to happen the way it unfolded.

The next day I made arrangements for an excellent massage therapist to work pulling his muscles back down from the knots they had made around his joints when they atrophied. She made a big difference! Then we had two people from his Maui Hui who were Hawaiian healers (worked in energy) and offered to come and work on him. They had to tell me to stop holding him in my energy because they needed to "get in" and work on him. I was relieved to let go and have someone else hold him in energy for a while. They then helped me afterwards. What a strain I had been under. I was able to relax with their work and center myself from the extreme pressure and stress I had been under.

What a relief to be away from that responsibility and pressure, if for just a little while.

He entered what he said was a "new thing for my life and I'm looking at building a better life". He had moved into Light! It was really the closing of the old and re-opening a new part of what began with our wedding. This solidified our knowledge that we are to be here on Molokai together, doing something for the community of Molokai and assisting others with their spiritual path.

CHAPTER THIRTY-EIGHT

MY FRIEND LEFT FROM MAUI TO return home, and Bill and I returned home to face his therapy and recovery alone. This was harder now because I didn't have her emotional support. We had some lovely friends who brought dinner. People would leave food for us. Some even left various items of fruits and vegetables and left them on the steps. We didn't even know who they were. His family never came by to see him or help me with his care.

Bill was getting good at moving from the bed to the wheelchair and back and took satisfaction with himself at his new found abilities. He kept pushing himself everyday like an athlete would do. He would go to the kitchen and pull himself up by the counters and stand. I was just amazed at the speed with which he improved. He had such an athletic body to begin with and he possessed such a strong mind, I shouldn't have been so surprised.

One day a Molokai musician and friend brought Bill a large bag of opi'i, which is a Hawaiian delicacy from the ocean. Bill used to dive for it all the time. He loved it. This friend had brought bags before, but this day, Bill gobbled them up as if he hadn't had any for years. After he finished half of the quart bag, I took it away so he wouldn't overdue on one food and put it up in the freezer which was above the refrigerator. He was angry at me for taking it away, so I went to bed to avoid any argument.

When I lay on my right side in bed, I could see the kitchen from our bed and particularly, I could see the refrigerator. Pretty soon, I heard the wheelchair and him getting into it. Then I saw the wheel chair coming into the kitchen and heading towards the refrigerator. I watched him open the refrigerator and look inside. Then he rolled his chair backwards and closed the door. Then I see the chair come up to the refrigerator again. Nothing happened for a few moments.

Then I saw him lift his legs with his hands and take his feet off the wheelchair foot supports and put his feet on the floor. Then amazingly ... he stood up and opened the freezer door to look for the opi'i!!!! I immediately got up and came out and we laughed at how I had tried and tried to get him to stand up on his own, but it was the opi'i that actually got him to do it!

Now that he could stand, I went about designing a trip for us to take in September (four months after the paralyses set upon him) so that he had something to look forward to and work towards getting in shape for. This was the psychological motivator he would need. The Colorado Bar promoted a trip to two areas of the world I had not been. He liked the idea of going on another trip, and I could tell he made up his mind to prepare to go, he would be walking soon and then we could go to the pool. Since his muscles atrophied, and he had been so sick, he had lost a lot of weight. He was down to 240 lbs. He needed to gain muscle back without gaining weight.

Now that he could stand, I had to work with him on walking with the walker. Soon he was able to do that, and although I rented the wheelchair for two months, I returned it within three weeks and the hospital bed also! When the hospital bed went, he came into our bed which was low and difficult for him to get in and out of, but we were at last in our bed together again side by side. That night we cried and cried – remembering all we had gone through and what a close call he had in the hospital. I knew he was out of the woods now. He knew he was not, and asked me if I could see who was sitting on the bed? I do not very often have the gift of sight and did not see. It was his (deceased) brother, he said.

He was using a walker but didn't like it. When we went to the community pool to start gaining muscle and walking, it was necessary for him to use the walker. He improved greatly within a short month or two. He was simply amazing in gaining his body movements back and strength again.

All during this recovery time, we were working on getting our homestead house completed also. The builder was recovering from his liver surgery and had assigned others to complete it. Meanwhile, Bill and I were trying to move out of a house he had lived in for twelve years. I was busy collecting boxes from the two grocery stores in town and packing up what I could. Bill was simply overwhelmed by the debris under the house that had accumulated for 12 years. Fortunately, our church once again came to help us and removed seven truck and trailer loads to the dump. They were given some of Bill's treasures also. It was empty under the house now! His machines needed to be moved to the shop/storage building at the new house by professionals with lifts because they were so heavy. I wanted to get into our new house by my birthday, and Bill bought cots for us to sleep on so we could.

Our trip was planned in September (my birthday month), and I had planned a week's visit to England which was my dominant ancestral culture. I felt that Bill, who was Hawaiian and who had brought me into the Hawaiian culture, needed to see that there were good qualities in my culture also; and we needed to go to the source to discover it. He would be broadened by travel like I was and start respecting other cultures different from Hawaiian and recognizing that there were other good people in the world other then Hawaiians and indigenous people. Traveling in other countries is enlightening, and brings tolerance to the consciousness with understanding and acceptance of others.

When you travel and understand how similar all cultures are, your preconceived prejudice against people because of skin color, race, or religion, melts away and out of you. All peoples' creation myths are similar as are their understanding of the world and their place in it. Their spirituality is linked to a Creator and their relationship with the Creator is how they live their lives.

CHAPTER THIRTY-NINE

THE DAY OF THE TRIP CAME and at the airport, I saw for the first and only time, Bill was afraid. He was afraid to go and leave the US on such a long trip being so tentative on his legs and fragile compared to how he used to be. He doubted he could do it. I looked him straight in the eyes and said, "Yes you can". We walked onto the plane and started the trip. It was a long one all the way to London, England -- half way around the world again and 12 hours time difference from Hawaii. As we got into the trip, he relaxed and became excited. I knew we would not be able to do as much as in our earlier travels, but he would be interested in everything around him, get 'out of himself' and learn about my culture.

During the flight across the Atlantic, he was gone from his seat a long time, and I thought maybe he was in the back of the plane just standing and stretching his legs. He finally came back and said, "You won't believe what happened". He explained he was in the loo and as he was zipping up, his wedding ring came off and went into the toilet!

He hunched down with his massive frame in those small lavatories on the planes in coach class, reached past the flapper in the toilet with his fingers and felt the ring on the edge just before the drop off into the big tank. He got up and went to the stewardess and told her what happened and told her, "My wife will kill me if I lose this ring".

She gave him a fork which he bent into a hook to try and snag the ring. She guarded the door so no one would come in when he was trying to accomplish this delicate feat. He did it! He came back

195

laughing and told me the story. The stewardess came by and joined in our laughter. I kept the bent fork, and still have it.

He hadn't worn a wedding ring...not even in his first marriage because of work. He had lost this ring on two prior occasions in the ocean while swimming. It is a very heavy ring because his fingers and hands are big and it falls off especially when his hand is outstretched while swimming. Both times in the ocean, he found the ring-- miraculously! This time he decided to tape and glue it on his finger. It didn't look so good and he wore it on the index finger of his left hand (instead of the 3rd finger), because with his weight loss it fit better on that finger. When we returned home, he super glued a small rope he placed around it to make the opening smaller. He was making sure it would not come off again. It didn't.

We landed in Heathrow around 9:30 p.m. their time, rented a car, it was raining and we needed to drive on the wrong side of the road again like in New Zealand. Bill was always the driver. He enjoyed that because cars were important to him. As a young man he had built cars and motorcycles from scratch including a model T Ford and had won many awards and trophies at car shows with it. It was no longer that important for me to be in control. I was just grateful to be taken care of and on this trip. We both learned a lot in the past year about control, and how we have no control over anything or anyone except our own thinking, attitudes and actions. We gave up trying to control anything in another's life.

I actually enjoyed having Bill drive as I enjoyed having him take care of me in all other ways too, to look after me, and to protect me. I had finally allowed myself to be pampered, cared for and loved. It was very comforting and a welcome relief from my other marriages. I could relax. It made me very happy. It was a big change for me in my life. I learned about trust again having had it early on before my Father died.

When we arrived and got settled in, we headed for Avebury one of our two most important destinations here. On the way we stopped at Marlboro, a charming medieval town where we ate lunch, and I bought Bill a hand made carved wooden cane as he was having some difficulty maintaining his balance as he walked.

With the cane he was able to walk without holding on to me, not that I minded that, but I felt, he needed to improve the use of his leg muscles and re-learn balance. He used it through out the first part of the trip and vastly improved everyday with walking. He was getting stronger and stronger. He forgot about his weak legs as he was walking while looking at everything around him new and exciting. By the end of our trip, he wasn't needing the cane at all.

Avebury's great stone circle is the best known and largest of 799 circles found in the United Kingdom. It is about 332 meters in diameter. Although first discovered in 1649 and presumed to be built in 2500BC, it had not been excavated to any extent until 1908 and beyond. Iwi (bones) were found and dated back to 2100BC.

Treasures come in many different forms throughout life. Bill and I treasured the sun sets, sun rises. stars at night, and of course, the ocean and mountains. Rocks, (pohaku) were important to both of us also. I took geology as my science in college and married a geologist, and Bill, because he was a spiritual Hawaiian, carried with him knowledge of all the Hawaiian significance surrounding pohaku.

We were very interested in the plethora of circles formed by rocks in England, and faces we found in the rocks. Avebury was the 'super bowl' of discovering faces in rocks. It was overwhelming the numbers you find. These ancient rocks stand as silent sentinels to our human heritage and the ancestors who have gone before. Who are the faces in them?

We were uplifted by Avebury and stayed quite a while. Our last name, Kapuni, means circle in Hawaiian and we found a spiritual connection for us and these ancient sacred stone circles we walked in England.

Among the rocks at Avebury

Our next stop over was the Old Manor Hotel in Bradford on Avon. This was a charming and elegant old bed and breakfast home with outstanding food. Its' clientele were mostly wealthy people from London trying to get away to the country for the weekend. We were the exception to their guest list.

We were always an exceptional couple to look at. I never realized it except when we were both in front of a mirror together. I completely forgot about our difference in skin color. Bill could be very dark at times. His skin was a gorgeous golden bronze naturally (like the kind of tan I tried to get all summer long with the sun tan lotions, coco butter, and baby oil), when he had not been in the sun and when his circulation was good.

I can't remember when I stopped noticing skin color in people. I learned to be afraid of dark skinned people, just like I was taught to be afraid of China and its people behind the bamboo curtain and the Russians behind the iron curtain. Through all my traveling around the world meeting people with many skin colors I realized there was no need to be afraid of them. You don't notice skin color, when you grow spiritually enough as to not feel the sense of 'differentness' between people but rather know that we are all one. You also transcend the false separations of superiority whether light skinned or dark skinned or vice versa and only see and feel the goodness in others. We made quite an interesting couple to look at in England as we had in that restaurant in Laramie, Wyoming.

We traveled down to Cornwall, because I remembered my grandfather saying that was where his ancestors were from. It was the rural portion of England and, as such, very different then the hubs and populated areas. We went to Lizard Point. I thought that appropriate since one of Bill's amakua is the lizard or mo'o. The roads were sandy and one lane with tall tall hedges grown up so that you couldn't see over them or ahead of you. We stopped at Cadgwith, a fishing village built on hills and watched men pull a large fishing boat up onto the shore by rolling it on logs. Bill got out of the car and walked around on the hill to take pictures and see better. He forgot he was recovering from paralysis.

This 'boot' of the country was interesting to Bill because it was predominantly fishing villages very quaint with lots of charm, pubs, boats, etc. It was cold at Land's end so he bought a cap he used throughout the trip. No need for knitted caps on Molokai.

Land's End I thought was where the ships for America left from; and, hence, perhaps this was where my grandfather's ancestors were from.

CHAPTER FORTY

W E WERE FORTUNATE TO BE BOOKED on one of the six tours that takes you right into Stonehenge which is a World Heritage Site, and the most outstanding prehistoric monument in the British Isles. Our whole trip was planned around this one day because the time to walk among the stones for the public is now limited to six times a year.

Some 7-8000 years ago, the Stonehenge area was pine and hazel woodlands. There then began a three phase building of the site that was in use thousands of years. Around 3050BC a circular ditch and bank (called a henge) was constructed at the place. Then 2600 BC a wooden structure was constructed at the center; and 2500-1500 BC a stone monument was constructed, land arranged and re-arranged over almost 1,000 years. These ancient people mapped the course of the sun and moon to build this monument.

The larger stones are called Sarsen stones (a very hard sandstone difficult for even modern steel tools to shape and weighing up to 50 tons each) and brought from about 19 miles away. A pair of Sarsen stones held up one long curved shaped lentil (stone) which contained two holes in it to fit over the raised knobs at the top of each of the upright Sarsen stone. The lentils were also joined to each other by a ridge on each end matching a groove on the next one. These methods of attaching and securing the stones are unique from all other prehistoric stone circles. In addition, all other prehistoric stone circles are not shaped and smoothed like the rocks at Stonehenge.

There are smaller stones called Bluestones that were brought from the mystical Preseli Mountains in Wales about 240 miles away. They are placed inside the horseshoe circle of the Sarsens.

The Bluestones were similarly joined as the larger circle of Sarsens but fewer remain. There is a circle of Bluestones placed around the inner horseshoe circle of Sarsens. In addition, at the bases of these monoliths, the stone hammers and tools used to shape the pohaku were now used to wedge around the base so they would be tight next to earthen holes dug and placed in the ground next to the stone to keep it from tipping over.

The entrance to Stonehenge was marked by two huge stones and the pathway leading to and from what was called the Avenue. The Avenue pointed to sunrise on the longest day of the year and in the opposite direction to the sunset on the shortest day of the year. It is presumed that Stonehenge was a temple used for worship maybe of the sun, or used for astronomy calculations; but it is not known for sure. Christian churches often point to the rising sun at the equinoxes but are not temples for sun worshiping or used for astronomy observations. What can be said is that it was used for a place of prehistoric worship or astronomy over a very long period of time at least -- seventeen centuries.

Bill and I felt the tremendous power and energy approaching it from the highway and when we were there. There were three different levels of energy we felt from the highway to the center of the circles. We felt very blessed that we were able to walk among these giant rocks and feel them. Bill correctly felt the burials all around. He pointed to the places people had been buried. I was impressed at Bill's sensitivity to the energy of the burials. I could not feel them. We always enjoyed sharing our spiritual awareness wherever we were. It was extremely difficult for us to leave the area. We were the last to go and were finally ushered out by security. It was a very spiritual and uplifting experience for us. You didn't even have to touch them to feel their power and feel the tranquility and strong centered power enveloping us.

We were obviously moved by the experience as was everyone, for there was silence in the bus for quite a while as we all felt the spiritual residue with us. We were leaving such an important area of Britain where many ancient stone circles were as well as many important churches like Salisbury Cathedral. In my opinion they were all congregated there for a reason... spiritual energy from the earth.

It was with sadness that we prepared to leave England. We had had such a good time and more importantly Bill had learned a lot about my cultural background and enjoyed, respected, and appreciated it. Exposure to different cultures broadens your outlook and brings you further understanding of the human race. Every culture has had disappointing and embarrassing and shameful times in their history, but we are all here to learn individually and as cultures, nations and races. We just try and do our best at every stage we encounter on our paths. We knew in our sadness we would not be returning for a stay here in England again.

CHAPTER FORTY-ONE

WE ARRIVED HOME ON MOLOKAI AND the first thing Bill wanted to do was see his grandkids. We drove over to their house on the way home from the airport to see them in time to see his son-in-law unloading a truckload of coconut stumps gathered from the King Kamehameha coconut grove below our house. They were for classes he intended to teach and produce 100 drums for a celebration of a Kumu recently deceased. This was the first Bill had heard of this! Bill was the Kalai Pahu meaning the Master Pahu maker and according to Hawaiian protocol, everything that was to be done in the Hawaian culture surrounding the Pahu, was to go through him first. This was a huge breach of Hawaiian protocol, let alone a backstabbing of the family Kapuna, and disrespecting the Kumu Bill Kapuni.

We were then invited to a meeting about this project after everything was apparently already decided, while we were on our rehabilitation trip. We attended one meeting where his adopted daughter, son-in-law and ex-girlfriend attended along with some others. This went all right, although Bill made it clear that he would be the supervisor of all activity and teach some also. In Hawaiian culture, whatever the Kumu says, particularly the Kalai Pahu, that is what is to be done. There was a second meeting scheduled.

Between these meetings Bill was attempting to get assistance from his son-in-law and daughter with the move to our new home as it was not completed before we left on our trip. Finally one Saturday they came for a few hours and helped move two truck loads to the new house. His daughter helped some, and I gave her the choice of lots of kitchen dishes and appliances I had from my condo and other items some of which she wanted but did not return to take; so they were given to others who subsequently helped us.

There was a second meeting called and after approval of many corrections to the minutes from the previous meeting, Bill's son-in-law said he "was tired of always being #2 and wanted to be #1"! Imagine! This young man was not native Hawaiian, had not finished his training, did not have the cultural sensitivity and knew nothing of Hawaiian culture and protocol; and he wants to take Bill Kapuni's place! He showed an inexcusable disrespectful attitude towards his kumu and kupuna, Bill Kapuni. With that Bill looked at his daughter and said "You are not my daughter. I have no family". He got up and walked out. I was so surprised my mouth dropped open. I knew that when he said something he meant it. There would be no going back. This was the last straw. He had enough of their disrespect towards him. He looked over his shoulder at me as if to say, are you coming. I quickly got up and followed him.

This was the final blow given by his daughter to him that broke any cord that might still remain between them. He never felt the same about them after that evening. All the nasty things they had done and continued to do, could ever touch the hurt done to this cultured Hawaiian Pahu Kumu that evening. She was not Hawaiian. She was not his daughter.

We went and prayed at the Vertex at sunrise the next day and the next. The answers he received from the prayers culminated in a letter of resignation from him and I to the group spelling out all the deception surrounding the meetings, pilikia, and what went on before the meetings, in Hawaiian the term is -- not pono. He specifically stated that his son-in-law could no longer use his name as his kumu in any resume for any wood carved drums or art he may make in the future.

From almost the beginning of our marriage, Bill asked me to adopt a child with him. He said he wanted a family with ME. We always regretted not being together sooner so we could have biological children together because we thought they would turn out to be very special. But, we were not ready to meet each other earlier. I did not join his desire to adopt at that time, because we were newlyweds with adjustments to make between ourselves first and cultures second. Then life happened along the way as you have seen. We put it off, but it was never out of Bill's mind. He brought it up often and told his daughter and son-in-law about his intention to adopt even two children he said one time!

Now, after this backstabbing I felt we needed to adopt. We began to apply several places. We even went so far as the finger printing, criminal background check, and recommendations from friends. It was an elaborate process, but we put forth the effort because it was his wish. I did feel that having a child around would elevate his mood and bring more joy into his life like I had observed his granddaughters did for him. Bill was a man who thoroughly enjoyed children all his life and enjoyed teaching them. Bill had had eight foster children. It was the Hawaiian way to have big families. For whatever reason, both of us seemed destined to not be surrounded with children or grandchildren. Perhaps it was a sacrifice for the Spiritual path we had chosen for ourselves.

Halloween came and went. No grandkids. Bill had disowned his daughter in public, and I knew there would be no Thanksgiving either; so we flew to Kona and visited Bill's cousins for a most enjoyable time. We watched their old childhood movies with pictures of Bill and his Tutu, aunties and Mom who all helped raise him. While there we interviewed with an adoption agency and he went to relatives looking for children. None were forthcoming.

Before Christmas we decorated the house while thinking about and hoping the granddaughters would be able to come and see us and receive the presents we had gotten for them on our trip. No kids, but the house looked so magical we decided to share it with some friends and entertained a little before my brother came for Christmas and after they left as well.

I always loved Christmas. It was always a very special time of year for me. Even during the 'dimly lit years in my life", I would always enjoy the spirit of Christmas and enjoyed giving. It was a time that I felt light inside me. I remember the years I bought gifts for people that took me until March to pay off on the credit card. Every year I would bake cookies and make candies and give them away in tins at Christmas to friends and neighbors. I enjoyed the giving and bringing joy to people.

My brother and his wife came for Christmas and we had a wonderful time…lots of laughter, because my brother is very funny. He and Bill liked each other a tremendous amount. They are both likable men. For New Years, they set off fireworks they had bought and acted like little boys. I think fireworks does that to men….makes them little boys again and that is why they like them so much. For me, they are just loud, very loud, but pretty, nevertheless.

The very few fights we had were always about his eating the amounts and types of food Bill consumed. We had come almost full circle from when I was in the accident and injured so badly and he took total care of me in all ways until now. He still took care of me spiritually and emotionally, but he was not able to do what he used to do physically. It was hard for him to get out of chairs and even walk. We had reversed roles. I was the caregiver now.

Bill and I sat on the couch New Year's night, his arm around me, and we talked about the future and what he was eating. I noticed he had been putting on weight since we came back from our trip and he hadn't been able to see his grand daughters. During the trip, he was walking and moving well and, although gaining a little weight with all that great food, not a significant amount. We had a very serious discussion, sitting on the couch in each other's arms, about his weight and heath. He said he would try better in '08 to eat better and less of it. With that conversation, we fell asleep in each other's arms sitting on the couch. My brother woke us up about 2:00 am. My brother was quite taken by that sight and later shared to me "very few people ever get what you and Bill have". We both knew that.

Will and I put on a birthday party for Bill. It was a lovely party. In addition to food delicacies, some guests brought gifts also. Some of the La'au activists brought him a wall hanging made from driftwood and shells and glass all collected from La'au Point for they often stayed there to maintain the occupation. It remains outside our front door. I can always hear the wind come up from the mountains when it moves and jingles against the wall.

CHAPTER FORTY-TWO

Bᴇᴄᴀᴜsᴇ ᴏғ ᴛʜᴇɪʀ ɪɴᴛᴇɴᴛɪᴏɴᴀʟ ᴍɪsʟᴇᴀᴅɪɴɢ FACTS (illustrated in my table and intentionally omitting my table from their answers), rather then being the first subdivision denied approval by the Commission, the Ranch withdrew their first EIS submission and submitted their second EIS to the Land Use Commission. Comments and questions were due February 22. During our entertaining over the holidays someone connected to one of Ranch's staunch political supporters asked me if I would consider $40K for not submitting questions this second time. I was so shocked and angry that someone would even think that I could be bribed, I could not answer. I answered in my mind by telling myself I'd ask even more questions then before even though this EIS was larger and different from the previous one and had to be completely re-read and questioned all over again.

Since Bill was spending so much of his time resting now, he didn't mind my incessant work on the word processor for this project as he did the year before when he was still raring to go and full of energy. We had sacrificed time together then when I was tied to the computer with a brain injury. I was surprised at how much easier this time was for me then the last. I had, indeed, improved the workings of my brain and found new pathways with which to think. I could actually remember and comprehend better and focus longer.

As always when I approached the machine, I prayed and asked the La'au spirits to guide me for I would have no time to proof read the 5,000 questions I intended to write with the time restriction of 30 days and my dyslexia. I worked round the clock for twenty-nine days while Bill cooked for me when I was hungry and prayed for me also to receive guidance. I would work, eat, and sleep when I couldn't think anymore. By February 11, when we were going to Honolulu for the day to attend Bill's sister-in-law's funeral services, I was able to print off and copy four sets of 3,500 completed questions for the Ranch. I wanted to get that much filed in Honolulu so that they would be in and completed and off my mind. I did that.

Upon our return home that same day, the dogs were out of the house running around in the yard, and the gate to the decks had been opened. When I went inside to the dinning room table were my papers were, the two envelopes containing the 3,500 questions were each missing one section of questions. They were complete sets ready to send off to the appropriate authorities, but they were now each missing one of the three sections of the questions. Did someone think that I would just send off the envelopes without rechecking their contents?

I asked my friend who had Xeroxed the copies for me if she was sure she made four complete sets? She said yes. She was positive. I had hidden the forth set for my copy in the house separate and away from the mass of papers on the table before I left, just to be safe. I found that fourth set complete and then was certain someone broke into the house to find and take questions. My keys were also missing from the glass bowl they had been in on the dinning room table. A couple days later I was told that the Ranch was thinking of throwing in the towel...they must have known about the 3,500 questions I had already submitted for this second round!

I wasn't finished with my questions, yet. I still had 10 more days to post mark the envelope. I diligently began to work some more. I had gone through the most difficult material—their Appendixes (some of which had been changed and/or updated) and which contained legal type documents and all the expert's documents. I actually fell short of my goal and ended up submitting only a total of 4912 questions for the Ranch to answer on their EIS before they could proceed further before the Commission. This was my answer to the offer of $40K – 4912 questions!

I am grateful for my guidance in accomplishing this task for it was important to the survival of the Hawaiian culture on this

Island. I was blessed for having been a trial attorney used to writing interrogatories and questions for cross-examination of witnesses. I set up my questions to catch misinformation and lies. It would take ONE attorney just as long or longer to answer the questions to avoid conflicting answers then it took for me to draft them.

If the development had been approved, not only would homesteaders, who are allotted 2/3rds water resources on Island, have lost significant amounts of their future allotment (for the Ranch would be using 4million gal/day of water); but, the traditional Hawaiian lifestyle on Island would have been abolished like no night fishing, no boats on reef, limited number of fish allowed to catch, permits given only after education classes (knowing one half the Island is illiterate) and beach access by permit only. This shoreline access management plan would have changed how native Hawaiians and people on Island would be able to use their natural resources on the coastline of La'au Point, which is the richest fishing around the Island.

CHAPTER FORTY-THREE

Bill BEGAN 2008 WITH THE INTENTION and determination to work on the pahu for the Canoe Festival, but his son-in-law had taken all the coconut stumps available on Island from the Kamehameha Coconut Grove below our house. This was not Hawaiian culture—to exhaust a resource to the point of depletion. Hawaiians always took only what they needed and no more. This kept the resourse sustainable and available for all to share. He wanted to make pahus to sell to the tourists. Some of Bill's friends brought over a large stump for him to carve for the festival with a front end loader, and Bill began working on it. His plan was to work a little everyday until he would get tired. He started out working four hours a day and then by the end of February it was down to two.

February came and Bill remembered Valentines Day's and went out to get me flowers and drew a hand made card; even though by this time, he was moving very slowly and having a great deal of trouble with his pain. We had a wonderful Valentine's celebration – just the two of us. We were 'allowed' to finally (after 5 months) see the granddaughters February 17th for one hour to have 'Christmas" with them. It was nice to see them, but he was very tired by then. I was holding him every day in my energy field. I didn't realize that unlike the healings I did for people where I worked solely as a conduit for God's energy, for Bill I was also giving my life force energy to him, and my energy was leaving me. Puna made a surprise visit for the day and brought one of the halau and two friends from Europe with her.

Puna said she came over from Kauai for the day because she was worried about MY health. I thought she came over to help me with Bill because she was a healer also. She shared with me that my energy was disappearing from her vision of me, and if I didn't stop giving to Bill I would go first. I told Bill and we talked about me pulling back my energy. He had been failing in his strength and energy level, and I had picked it up for him with mine. We talked about both going together, but he wanted his projects completed, and I shared the one thing I needed to do before I leave…that I was to reunite with my son and grandson so my son could forgive himself and live a happier life. He promised me he would pick up the slack when I started pulling back my energy that was holding him now. But, he was unable.

When I started withdrawing my energy, he began doing less and less, like not even taking off his shoes before he entered the house. It was too much of an effort for him to lean over and remove his tennis shoes. Bill was working on the drum only two times a week in March. He began working on cleaning and clearing out his truck and organizing the container and going through things in the workshop. I should have known he was preparing to leave then, but I couldn't allow myself to see it. It would have been too awful for me to see. I just lived moment by moment.

We were spending a lot of time in spirit and praying and being quiet. He even stopped looking at the TV and we began talking and sharing all over again like we did when we first met. Learning from each other and loving each other completely, unconditionally in light.

He used to speak about time and how there is no time in spirit only the now. He would work on small projects on the porch like carving mo'o on bone joints from animals, and we would watch the trees and ocean from the lani, and he would take naps outside in the recliner. He was able to do less and less. He wouldn't go to the store or the post office with me anymore, although most Saturday mornings I would wake up and he would be gone. I never asked where he had been, thinking he went to the ocean or wharf. One Saturday, as I came out on the lani to greet him as he drove up, because he had been gone longer then usual, he told me. "If I'm ever not here when you wake up, go to the wharf. I'll be down there."

One of 'our things' was to go to the local Hotel Molokai on the weekends Friday or Saturday night and dance. We liked to dance together under the stars. I loved it particularly because we were outside by the ocean under the swaying palms, looking at the moon and stars and listening to the beautiful music.

We often danced at home also because we played lots of music either the 'oldies' on radio or Hawaiian music on CDs. Our favorite songs were "When a Man Loves a Woman" and "n dis Life" from the CD entitled IZ The Man and His Music in Concert. We would sing the lyrics of this song to each other as we danced.

> "For I've been blessed in my life
> There was an emptiness within.
> I was imprisoned by the power of gold
> With one kind touch you set me free
> Let the world stop turning
> Let the sun stop burning,
> Let them tell me love's not worth going through
> If it all falls apart
> I will know deep in my heart
> The only dream that mattered had come true
> In this life, I was loved by you.
> For every mountain I have climbed
> Every raging river I have crossed
> You were the treasure that I lived to find
> Without your love I would be lost
> I know that I won't live forever
> But forever I'll be 'loving you."

Bill and I

CHAPTER FORTY-FOUR

MARCH SAW ME LEAVE FOR HONOLULU by myself because he was unable to go to both Prince Kuhio Day on the 26th in Honolulu and cook for the fund raiser on Molokai for our Homestead association on the 29th. His Kalamaula Mauka Homestead Association was very important to him and he wanted to make sure there was money for the organization, because he and I had been subsidizing it so often in the past few years with no fund raising activity. This was the first time since we went on that first trip to the US together before we were married that we had been apart. This one night we sacrificed for his Hawaiian Homestead Association.

It was strange for me to not be sleeping next to him. We had been together almost every minute since before our marriage. It was very strange for both of us. Earlier, I had gone to Kauai for my halau retreat which Puna was holding and spent only the day, because he did not want me to be gone over night. I understood and complied with his wish as I didn't want to be away from him either.

I couldn't accept that he was slowing down so very much. I didn't want to accept it. Denial was a defense mechanism I had used during my life off and on to protect myself from pain. Every time he was sick before, he would recover and bounce back to be with me. He had been living with 14% kidney function for over one year now. We were spending time more and more alone and in spirit and drawing closer and closer in our commitments to each other for eternity.

He found someone who he paid to help him with the yard cleanup and cutting and collecting Bougainville from a local church yard, because he was unable to do it himself. He planted almost 300 cuttings for later planting around the perimeter of our one acre

214

property to form a fence around the land. He had many plans for the property. He watered and cared for those plants. I asked him once why are you spending so much time on the plants and not the drum? He didn't answer me. I should have known then, but I couldn't allow myself to see it in my consciousness. Why are you cleaning out the truck? Why are you cleaning up the shop? Why are you sitting down in the chair when you came up the steps? He replied "resting". I could not process and accept what was happening. I could not.

He started telling me how much he loved me stopping me in the middle of the great room placing his hands on my shoulders to get my attention and looking down into my eyes and saying "No matter what anyone ever says, I never loved anyone but you. Remember that." I said I will. That was confusing for me because it was unusual for him to say "never loved anyone but you". He did it a second time. I should have known then, but I thought it might be because of our deepening love in our relationship. One night while we finished up playing cards, he said "You know what's happening don't you?" I said, "no, what?" We both looked away. I was unable to talk about it and face it. I was intentionally denying what I felt he was going to say; because I didn't want to hear it. I couldn't accept it; it was too much for me to bear. How could I be loosing what I had looked for my whole life?

He called his son-in-law a few times to ask him for help with the drum he had started for the festival, but his final effort of making things Ho-opono-pono, (a Hawaiian way of making relationships at peace) was met with no reply. They simply did not honor him as a father, kumu, kapuna, or Kalai Pahu. When people apparently told them Bill wasn't doing well, his daughter sent her husband to go see him one night the first week of May. He brought Bill a coconut for the milk inside is known to help kidney disease. She did not send the grand children nor did she call or come herself.

Bill then called his friend, who was the man who had brought him the coconut stump to help him finish the drum. I continued to do the errand running and cooking, but he didn't like my cooking very much now. He really only liked Hawaiian food now, and we were fortunate that some friends provided some for him, although he didn't eat that either.

Friday evening, May 9th, we had a nice family time together with some friends and their children stopping by. Bill couldn't come out to the table for dinner and wouldn't eat anything, but I put a shirt on him and everyone came back in the bedroom to see him. Bill particularly enjoyed spending time with their children. He loved children and loved to talk story with them. He wanted them all to carry on the culture and to be proud of who they are.

Saturday morning Bill's friend came over to help him with the drum as requested. I went back in the bedroom to tell him, but he was unable to get up and out of bed to work and told me to send him home. We spent the day quietly in spirit together. I still couldn't register the free fall decline Bill was in. I kept reading the Bible throughout the day and massaging his feet and legs gently...living in the moment.

We believe mana is the life force flowing through all living things in nature and us. The force flows from God and we spend our lives here searching for it. When you search within, you can find God; and as you find God, you find yourself in the process. (God, Ke Akua, Light, Spirit, Universe, Creator, Life Force, and similar names all refer to the same God in my mental, emotional and spiritual framework.) Both Bill and I lived in the now which is the only space you can find God and no where else in time. As you become one with the supreme force and the light shines through you and all around you, you are in spirit. We spent most of the day when Bill was awake, in spirit.

CHAPTER FORTY-FIVE

IT BEGAN ON MOTHER'S DAY. WE had been invited to a mother's day party, but I knew we would not be able to make it. Bill got up to go to the bathroom and fell. I couldn't get my giant of a Hawaiian husband up by myself. I tried the neighbors, but they were not helpful so my friend (having the party) sent five men over to help.

They easily picked him up, carrying him to a chair I had placed in the shower so that I could wash him off. They then lifted him back to the bed and left. He kept trying to sit up and not lie down and was despondent. I could not get him to answer my questions and became worried. We both had directives to die at home under hospice care, but my fears overcame me. The fear that maybe, this time, the medical profession could do something for him that I couldn't, and I'd be sorry if I didn't at least give the medical people a chance to help him. I finally told him if he didn't answer me I'd have to take him to the hospital. He said "No!" I still allowed fear to take over and I called the fire department.

Two yellow fire trucks came along with an ambulance. About twelve came up to get him and all shook his hand. He was friends with all of them. During the hand shaking, he looked at me and said, "Why did you do this?" I felt horrible and wondered why myself, knowing what our wishes were, to die at home; and I felt guilty for getting him to the hospital. I was hoping their medicine could do something for him. Even with my Christian Science upbringing and our own belief system, I didn't want to let him go if there was something medically that could be done.

When we arrived at the hospital, his blood pressure was 56 over 20 and they told me he could die any minute. I was asked about directives and told them, but I broke down and began to cry ferociously. I pleaded with Bill not to leave me. His BP suddenly came up and then they wanted to send him to Honolulu. He again looked at me and said "Honolulu?" in disbelief that I would send him there.

In Honolulu ER they said the same thing…he could die any minute. Then I began to try and get him home, because I was beginning to accept the words they were telling me 'he can go any minute' by allowing them to sink in and not deny it or try my prayerful way to heal him as I had several other times previously. Now, my campaign and battle cry was only to get us home to Molokai so he could die on Molokai in his own bed, which is what he wanted. They wouldn't let us leave the ER but put him in ICU, where they were going to poke him and do all kinds of tests on him all over again.

One doctor said that we couldn't leave because he was too unstable. At that point his former doctor, who had recognized something special about Bill, and knew he was a Kahuna, said they couldn't do anything for him. My response was "please make sure we get him home today. I have to get him home today". He said he would. He understood the importance for Bill to be in his home. I asked how long he would have, and he replied, "With a man like him, he will choose his own time."

I felt badly that we had lost 15 hours in the hospital and traveling to and from Honolulu. I had taken my Bible with me and read to him a lot, but hours of our private time left together, was lost. The good thing was that with Bill in Honolulu I was able to call his brother, Eddie's wife and sister, who could then all say their good-byes. They all came to the hospital and were very glad they were able to see him once again. His brother stayed until we were finally able to leave.

When we arrived home, two fire trucks were waiting in the yard lined up facing the house as if in tribute to this great Hawaiian they all loved as the ambulance pulled in; and about twelve men helped carry him into his bed to say their farewells. He felt better in his own bed and the dogs kissed and greeted him. It was a happy homecoming for the four of us.

The dogs had been like our children. They were most often with us. He used to take them to town with him in the car and Loke would sit in the front seat like a person. We spent hours and hours watching them play before us at the beach, in the ocean, in the yard, at the Vertex everywhere. They would bring smiles to our faces as they raced and tumbled across and over each other in their romping.

His son-in-law drove up in his truck to finally do some work. I told him what had happened. He was in disbelief because he had seen him only days before bringing the coconut, and now Bill was home with hospice. I welcomed he, his wife and the granddaughters to come and visit him later. They came back at 7:00 pm with pizza and this was only the second nice family time we had together ever. They came with aloha in their hearts for the first time!

I was surprised Bill was so forgiving and loving. He gave his daughter a chance to be pono. He asked her "How do you feel about your Dad dying?" She said, "Sad". He continued, "I'm here now. If there is anything you would like to say or talk about or ask questions about, I am here." She responded, "I have nothing to say Dad". He was giving her a chance to free herself of guilt and become pono with him. I knew how her answers hurt him and touched his shoulder for comfort. He then said to her, "You know, I had eight other children before you". She said she knew. (He had eight foster children.)

The next morning, before they came back, Bill and I had a wonderful time loving each other. Except for his weakness, it was like old times, playful, loving, joyful in the now without any illness, pain or anything but us together loving each other in spirit….God's love. We had such a magic touch for each other…like fireworks going off when we kissed and held each other. I was so grateful for that time.

Sometime after noon, the grand daughters and their parents, returned and stayed 7 hours this time taxing him greatly by the length of their visit. He and I slept a good deal through their visit. They finally left around 9:30 pm, and he began to have labored breathing, and I called the kahu for prayers and held the phone to Bill's ear so he could hear him. He listened intently and relaxed and started breathing normally again. Then we began going through the dark tunnel that night together.

CHAPTER FORTY-SIX

As WE LIVED IN THE MOMENT, embracing the precious here and now, I felt like we were about to endure a journey together. It felt as if I was being enveloped by a film surrounding us….there was only the two of us within the envelope of soft hazy air. We were in slow motion and we were the only two people in the universe. We were together with God in the now.

That night I started to swab out his mouth from the blood that was rapidly bleeding out from his body. He began to growl and bite at the air. Then I raised my arm and waved fiercely at whatever he was seeing (I could not see) but I felt their energy and told them "get back, get out of here, you are not wanted here". He stopped biting and growling because they retreated. I was the warrior he told me I had to be to marry him!

He then sat up and refused to lie down and sat on the bed looking at the floor hunched over. He had strength overpowering me and preventing me from getting him to lie down. I was worried he was going to wear himself out. I was able to get him to lay down twice and both times he pushed me right back up again with uncanny strength like the strength I remembered he had in New Zealand long ago before he became sick. He wanted to sit on the side of the bed, hunched over, hands clasped, feet on the floor, eyes closed, rocking and non-responsive to my questions. He refused all morphine, and became angry if I tried to give him some. He said he wanted to be alert at all times.

I just sat next to him trying to persuade him to lie down and touching him and rubbing his back and neck to make him feel better. I stayed up with him holding him, protecting his back, hugging him and wiping away the blood sometimes dripping from his mouth and nose. He wasn't speaking, but I knew he wanted comfort from me and needed me to stay awake with him. For some reason at 3:30am, I simply couldn't stay awake any longer. I told him I couldn't, I was fading. I stayed with him as long as I could because of the words he had said "ring of fire" and "hard even for me", terms spoken of for a kahuna's death, but my eyes were closing. I was exhausted and was falling asleep.

Because of our knowing each other very well and him often saying he never talked to anyone like he talked to me before, I knew a little of what he was talking about. I curled my body around his hips and backside encircling and protecting him with my body while he went through his kahuna warrior's battle, and I, protecting him as best I could in my sleep.

I was awakened by a motor noise from a car. It was Bill. He was rocking back and forth. I immediately got up and went around the bed to see what was happening. Blood was everywhere—on him, the bed, the floor. He appeared to be driving a car with his hands on the steering wheel and shifting gears with his foot on the accelerator and clutch. I said "Moto, Moto", the name his tutu called him when he was very young, and he came back into this reality responding to my energy and words. I held him while blood was running out his nose and mouth and onto my shirt and hair and legs. His legs and arms were covered in blood, and I sat in front of him to support his chest with my head as he was sitting on the edge of the bed. I was afraid he might fall off.

He kept trying to put our heads together so our crown chakras would be touching, but his head was too heavy for my small neck to support his head and his leaning body weight, and I couldn't do that for very long and told him so. He immediately stopped trying. He was always very considerate of me particularly physically when he was so much more powerful than I. By responding quickly to my request, I knew he could hear and understand what I was saying so I told him "I love you". He said "I love you". Those were the last words he ever spoke.

I just held him and calmed him and wiped the blood from his nose and mouth. His eyes were rolled back in his head and a white 'film' covered his eyes so you could only see a shadow of his iris and pupils and then his eye lids mostly closed. All the while I was holding him propping his chest up with my head so he wouldn't fall over.

Because he was sitting on the very edge of the bed precariously, and I was afraid he might slip off, I needed help to move him. I didn't want anyone to see him like this. I called his son-in-law, not the hospice nurse, and told him not to bring the children. I didn't want them at their tender ages to see and remember this horrific picture of their Papa. When they came, his daughter ran out of the room and gagged out in the kitchen, I chased out of the bedroom one of the grand daughters they had brought against my instruction.

I called the hospice nurse and the four of us were able to move him back to a comfortable laying position on the bed propped up with pillows behind his head and shoulders to make his breathing easier. The oxygen equipment still had not arrived.

He would bite the swab when I would try to swab out his mouth, because he thought I was trying to give him morphine. When I explained I was only trying to get some blood out, he would loosen his bite and allow me to enter his mouth. He was alert at all times, he just couldn't talk or move. I am not sure if he could see in the physical sense but surely in the spiritual sense.

The rest of Wednesday was uneventful except his BP and pulse were up and his kidneys were working beautifully – discharging 1500ccs. We had an oxygen machine and his breathing was better… not labored I became hopeful.

On Thursday morning, the hospice nurse told me I had to let him go. He wouldn't go unless I told him it was all right. On Thursday afternoon when all was quiet, he was peaceful, and we were alone, I teared up and started speaking to him about leaving – how I didn't want him to leave, but if he had to it would be OK. I would understand. He acknowledged what I said with a large tear dropping from his right eye as I was speaking through my own tears. He didn't want us to part either. By Thursday evening, I saw what I perceived a turn-a-round. His color was good. That beautiful golden tan color was back again, and I even called his brother to let him know he was doing better.

CHAPTER FORTY-SEVEN

Friday came with a bad sign. I was in the bathroom and they came. They were coming and going in the house whenever they pleased now without calling as if it was their house, and the hospice nurse noticed and mentioned it also. Strange when before this Monday, except for two times, they had not been to the house in the previous 8 months. When I made it to the door, they were all down at their car ready to leave, but the granddaughters ran up the stairs to the porch and entered the house immediately when they saw the door open. I asked them "What's wrong with your parents?" No reply.

The hospice nurse had just left after taking his vitals. I warned them that Bill was very weak today, and I asked them all to be very quiet. They entered, and I was handed the baby to hold. Why was I given the baby now when I had never been allowed to hold her before I did not know. His daughter dashed past me back to the bedroom like she owned the house; slamming the door which separated the bedroom area from the living area of the house with a loud noise I thought would hurt Bill in his precarious condition now. When I came back in the bedroom, she left not only the bedroom, but the house also, taking the baby and one of the girls, leaving only one girl and her husband behind.

I told the son-in-law the plan for completing the drum and requested he return a tool (a drummel tool) he had taken during the week whereupon he started with great disrespect yelling and swearing viciously at me. I asked him to leave, because I wanted everything peaceful for Bill. He wouldn't leave when I asked him to, so I had to call the police to have him removed.

225

A week or two ago, Bill had carved his amakua, a shark, on a special pohaku, which laid next to three healing stones near the house to protect me and the house. I had noticed a drilling noise while I had been at Bill's bedside during a visit of his daughter and her husband two days prior. I didn't think much of it at the time.

Bill's daughter (after receiving a phone call from her husband saying "the bitch called the police") came back at the time the police were arriving, and shoved her way through the two officers and slammed the door shut to the bedroom area, even after I had told her Bill was very weak and everyone needed to be very quiet today. She went to his bedside, leaned over him, and started yelling at him over and over "I love you Dad". My mouth opened and I was very afraid what her yelling would do to my husband in his fragile condition. She flung herself past the policemen, who had followed her back to the bedroom and were trying to hold her back when she came at me yelling "I hate you haole bitch", (which was strange to me because she had no Hawaiian blood in her either), and she proceeded to shove me over a chair and into a mirrored closet door.

The police immediately grabbed her and escorted her out and as she glared back at me I said, "You aren't really angry at me. You are angry at yourself for how you have treated your father the last year and a half".

Fortunately, some of Bill's friends who had been connected to us on a spiritual level in what I call a flow of energy that flows above us, felt the trouble in the force because they came up the stairs just before the police left. Our pastor and his wife came and prayed over the two before the police escorted them off the property.

I hugged my friend for a long time, because I was shaken (trembling almost) from the attack. We talked in the living room and I recounted to her what had transpired. Her husband immediately went back to Bill and started rubbing him, because he had turned black from the outburst of his daughter and not being able to do anything to protect me. He thought Bill's veins had constricted as he tried to move, clench his muscles and defend me. That cut off his circulation.

I was so grateful for our friends coming just when they did, for I was pushed up a notch in anxiety, because physical fear was now piled on top of what I had been living with my husband leaving this world. This was just more dark energy to get rid of so his passing could be peaceful and into the Light.

Because of the events in the house, the hospice people Friday afternoon told me they no longer wanted to sit with me, but would be on call should I need them and would still drop by to take his vitals every couple hours. They did not feel safe, and I understood that. It was just another piece of darkness trying to interfere with Bill's peaceful transition. I simply pressed on alone by myself with the dogs now. Friday night was quiet and I was happy because I believed Bill would improve. I felt relief by his calm breathing. I even walked the dogs away from the house to the road for the first time in almost a week before Hospice left. As I descended the stairs I noticed a carved stick man warrior carved on the pohaku where Bill had put his amakua. It was a figure of a warrior with a spear intending to kill the shark.

—⟋⟋⟋—

As I lay next to him, I awoke to the sound of Bill's heavy breathing, looked at him and closed my eyes again. I opened them again, and he was not breathing. I immediately called the nurse and she was there in a few minutes. I laid next to him with his arm around me and my head on his chest. I hadn't been able to lie with him like that for a long time, because I didn't want to hinder his breathing with my head on his chest.

Bill had chosen the Hula Piko celebration and the opening day of the Maui Canoe Festival to depart this physical world. He had, indeed, chosen his time to leave as the doctor said he would.

I laid there for quite a while in shock. The dogs came up on the bed with us, and I finally started to cry. We laid there for an hour and a half, sleeping with him -- the dogs and me.

When I got up from our restful nap, together, I kept trying to reach out and feel him in spirit and was puzzled he had not come to me yet. I thought I heard him, but it was too faint to hear, but then all of a sudden, he shouted at me in my ear, "Victoria", and I smiled and sighed a sigh of relief he was alive and also with me still yet.

I went to the kitchen and got a large clean bowl, and filled it with very warm water in which I poured lotion; because his skin was so dry from dehydration. I went to find the one last handkerchief I had saved from my childhood for some reason. I knew the reason now. It was embroidered with red flowers on trees. I gathered some candle sticks and candles and then placed them around his bed.

I took that embroidered handkerchief my grandmother had given me and began washing him. I started around his nose and mouth where blood lay in some of his pores from the continual bleeding he had endured. I gently, lovingly and carefully cleaned his whole face and ears. I then washed his hair and brushed it smooth. I then wiped his arms and hands and fingers slowly, slowly, lovingly until his whole body was clean. It took about one hour to complete my washing of my husband.

Afterwards the dogs came up on the bed again and smelled him. Each licked his face and hands copying me washing him I suppose. Loke pushed up the quilt covering his foot with her nose to see and sniff his 'bad toe'. She always licked it and did one last time.

Because I was always talking about eyes and what ones looked like when they were in spirit with God, I looked at his lids and was afraid to open them for fear they were not in light. I clearly heard his voice telling me to open his lids to look. I slowly lifted his eye lids and gazed into his eyes, they were stunningly beautiful. The white film was gone. His eyes were more beautiful then I had ever seen them. They were a deep rich golden brown with gold flecks in them now with dramatic white spikes flashing forth from his pupils. As I looked, his eyes were deep in 3D –like looking into the universe. It was no wonder his eyes were extraordinary. He was an extraordinary spiritual being. He had gone to the Light!

I laid down on the bed again and the dogs got up again with us. I placed his arm around me again only this time, he said in my ear "I'm not in the body"; whereupon, I got up and felt relief. Ah, I don't have to protect him anymore.

The mortician arrived and both dogs got side by side at the entrance to the bedroom and fiercely growled and barked. They were not going to let anyone take him away again! I had never heard them growl like that before or since. The two men needed to back out, and I leashed them and put them in the other bedroom so the two men could get by. I took the dogs in the living room and we all three waited together and watched them wheel him out of the house in a black bag.

During the washing I had tried in vein to remove his wedding band with soap. He had glued on that rope so he wouldn't lose it. I tried and tried and could not. Even though I knew he was not in his body any longer, I was afraid I would hurt him. I called upon a friend who had come over to be with me, and she was able to get it off and give it to me.

I placed it on the middle finger of my left hand for a couple of days, but it fell off like it did for Bill. When it fell, he said "see it falls off". I smiled because he had a smile in his words when he said that. The second time it fell off , he said 'see', and I was concerned I might lose it.

During the night somehow his ring on my middle finger ended up on my ring finger on top of mine! It fit tightly so that it would not fall off anymore. I wore his wedding ring on top of mine for one and one-half years.

PART IV

CHAPTER FORTY-EIGHT

THE WEEK BEFORE BILL DIED, I asked him, "if you leave this place, who will take care of me?" His reply was, "Me". I thought to myself, 'yeah sure, how you going to do that?' He has!

Our friend to whom we are spiritually connected and, who knew through our spiritual connection, I was facing trouble with his daughter and son-in-law and came right over while the police were there, had told me he would be back Saturday morning at sunrise to help me purify the aina which had endured so much pilikia Friday. Hawaiians believe like Indian culture that a place needs to be purified after trouble has occurred. (The bad, negative, dark, energy has to be removed.) The Hawaiians use Hawaiian Sea salt and the Indians use sage.

I really didn't think he would make it for sun rise so I attempted to walk the perimeter of the land myself with the dogs on their leashes, and being freaked by Bill's death and a vicious wind, were wildly pulling me this way and that as I attempted to sprinkle the salt water from a koa bowl Bill had made. I took a Mojo from the center of a tea leaf in the bouquet of Hawaiian flowers Bill had bought me at the Saturday market almost two weeks before. I must have looked a sight splashing sea salt water and being pulled this way and that by the dogs, my hair whipping in the angry wind, which had been very angry since he died, and saying prayers to God probably for protection and help, but I really don't remember.

When I was three quarters done, he drove up. He had everything properly prepared according to protocol and was ready to walk with me the perimeter of the land. He told me to choose where we would start and walk behind him saying whatever prayers I wanted to say and he would say his. I put the dogs in the house and followed him saying prayers. Bill didn't need any prayers because he was out of pain and went to the Light already.

When we finished the first side, the sun had come up over the mountain, and my friend asked me to go in front of him and continue my prayers and he would follow. We rounded the next corner and started up the side of the land by the neighbor's fence. Bill had a lot of construction planks piled up near the fence, but one was lying flat on the ground leaving about 14 inches between it and the fence enabling me to walk on the grass not the plank that was made of Styrofoam and covered on both sides with a metal grid which looked uncomfortable to walk on with my slippers.

About half way walking beside the plank, I heard a lot of racket behind me and thought my friend must be walking on the grid. With a few more steps I stopped and turned around. The racket stopped when I stopped. I looked at his face and he looked at me and said "It's not me, see? I'm on the ground like you". I looked at where he was walking. He was on the ground. We looked at each other, and I turned around to continue the walk and the racket started up again. I paid attention to my prayers now and not the sound. It shortly stopped after I was several feet past that plank.

When we finished, we went upstairs and three friends came to help me bringing food. After eating, they started cleaning the great room for me. They did a spring cleaning job lifting rugs and moving furniture etc. It was amazing. All I could do was sit and stare out the window in shock. That's pretty much all I could do for a long time. When people asked me questions, they had to ask twice, and if I still didn't respond, they dropped it. I could tell someone was talking to me but the words didn't register or my ears couldn't hear them.

I pretty much walked around in another place withdrawn from here, and everyone else did everything. Hawaiians are wonderful that way. When they see someone in trouble, they pitch in as a team to help. It is their Aloha spirit towards everyone. Bill was like that. He would always help someone in distress by the road or in the water.

My friend related to me about his night. He had had trouble going to sleep. Sometime after midnight he awoke and could not fall back asleep. He went to his recliner and sat and said he knew when Bill passed. So it was relatively easy for him to do the proper protocol preparation for our cleansing of the aina and be at the house before sunrise.

In the late afternoon when we were all sitting on the lanai, he asked me to go inside with him. He said he had something to share with me. He related to me what had occurred during our walk of the perimeter of the land. He said when the sun came up, he saw in addition to our two shadows, a third. I asked him if the third shadow was big. He said, "Yes, it was Bill". He then asked me if I remembered him asking me 'to go first', I replied, "I did." He asked me if I 'knew why'. I said "no". He said, "It was because Bill wanted to walk behind you during the cleansing ceremony of purification of the land and protection for you. He asked me if I remembered the 'clatter noise on the plank' by the neighbor's fence. I said, "Yes". He said, "That was Bill walking behind you." He is telling you he will protect you and this land from now on.

Bill was alive in spirit and coming to some people in their dreams. Another friend was the first to dream about Bill. He told her to come and help me for the 'celebration' and organize it. She did. They all made sure I would not be alone. I was in an extreme state of shock not even depression yet. I was praying to God to let me die now. I had never done that before in my life. I had always been able to see the silver lining in things before no matter what it was. Not this time. All I wanted was to be with Bill. I didn't want to be here anymore without him.

Gently the friends took care of me and listened and comforted. I am unable to fully explain the beautiful hearts of the Hawaiian people towards helping someone when they need help. When I was married to Bill, I always felt I was in the background and only present in a supportive manner for him, but several people expressed to me that very first week that the community wanted me to stay on the homestead and on the Island.

They loved me too – not just because I was married to and had cared for Bill Kapuni.

CHAPTER FORTY-NINE

THE NEXT TWO WEEKS WERE A blur for me. The third night I moved back to our bed. Hoku had been sleeping where Bill had died every night…waiting for him to return. Loke and I had been sleeping on the couch for three nights unable to go back to our bed as yet. Hoku, Bill's dog, slept and continued to sleep in his place on the bed.

If it had not been for all the wonderful people who planned, organized, and decorated for the celebration and generally took care of me, I would have been lost for I really was not here. I was off in a spiritual world with Bill. We were adjusting to our physical separation and changes in communication through the veil. Because my amakua is the black raven, who travels between the worlds, I decided I wanted to be where Bill was – not here in the third dimension. Bill and I had become one during his leaving and pulling apart was almost impossible. I remember telling people that half of me was with him. Some of me still remains with him as well as some of him remains with me.

The day of the celebration, a good friend, took off work and came over from Oahu for the day and stayed the night with me. Puna flew in from Kauai with three of her halau. They immediately took over cleaning the house and kitchen for guests, while Puna made me take a shower and change my clothes and fixed my hair on top of my head. She said I should dress for the celebration as if I were going out on my first date with Bill.

I don't know what I would have done had these friends not come. I was simply lost that day of the celebration. It was the most difficult day I have ever been through to be so brimming over inside with pain, shock, and grief; and yet, needing to keep my composure because Puna said if I am OK, others will be also; so I had to stay calm so they could. I was truly lifted up by all the aloha spirit people brought for both Bill and me.

My brother came out in a few days after Bill left to stay for a couple weeks. Everyone was relieved I would have someone to stay with me. Looking back on it, I was relieved also. My brother is always there for me when I need him.

The Chief of the Tahitians, three New Zealand carvers, the Executive Director and her assistant came over across the channel from the Maui Canoe Festival for the celebration and shared in the eulogy which lasted hours before, during, and after a traditional Hawaiian luau for 200.

The New Zealand carvers dedicated and named the canoe they had just carved at the Festival to Bill. They kept him in their prayers at all times during their circle and awa ceremonies with an empty chair where he would have been at the Canoe Festival. They carved him at the back of the canoe playing the Pahu and named the canoe after him "Pahu from Heaven". They all spent the night in our home and were amazed at the great variety of pieces found in his art. He wasn't just a pahu maker or a canoe builder. He created and carved everything Hawaiian.

New Zealand canoe

I spoke at the eulogy portion of the celebration, "Although, my husband. William Kua mo'o Helelani Kealoha Kapuni was a giant among men in all ways, he lived his human experience as a humble man. He lived in spirit and spread great aloha to everyone who made his acquaintance. He told me not to cry for he will be in the stars, wind, ocean and land. He did not want a funeral, he wanted a celebration of his life for he did not die."

A Honolulu TV news anchor sent two documentaries he had made of Bill Kapuni diving on the Backside of Molokai and making a Pahu Drum. They were shown along with a power point a local friend put together. The anchor said he can not think of Molokai without thinking of Bill Kapuni. His death announcement was broadcast on all state news programs.

I continued, "I knew Bill and I would always be together. Death is but a crossing much like crossing the sea. He lived his life first and foremost as a Hawaiian and shared his culture with Hawaiians and non Hawaiians alike. There would never be another Hawaiian like him", and those who came to celebrate his life knew that also.

That's why I asked for and received a beautiful celebration of his life, Hawaiian style with the second half of the program devoted to a Christian program that included hula and Hawaiian music also. After the blowing of the pu to begin the Hawaiian protocol ceremonies with a special pahu hula group along with Hawaiian stories, chants, male dancers and more hula. I stated, "I have my husband with me and always will, but the real loss from his death is to the Hawaiian culture".

I said at the eulogy "my husband had humble beginnings from which he grew and expanded his endeavors through creating cars and motorcycles out of metal and then painting them to make them beautiful objects of art. When he returned to Hawaii and went into woodworking in earnest, he expressed his great mana through his Hawaiian art.

"The lesson we can learn from this highly creative and intelligent man's life is that we don't know who we are until we see what we can do. How fortunate we all were to have known him, learned from him and enjoyed him as he flashed that big smile our way. We each can be glad for the experience of knowing Bill Kapuni in whatever manner that was. Treasure those moments you had interacting with him and hold them dear to your heart. Celebrate the life of this beautiful Hawaiian man for there will never be another Hawaiian like him."

"Bill often spoke of time moving on a continuum and that the horse carriage of the past can't go anywhere in the future. Over the last weeks of his life we found peace when time doesn't matter or exist anymore. Time for us became a moment that lasted forever.

What a joy life becomes where there is no time."

CHAPTER FIFTY

W HEN THE EXECUTIVE DIRECTOR SPENT THE night
of Bill's celebration at our home, she asked me to attend the Maui
Canoe Festival final events of the parade, canoe launching and
farewell dinner to be held in a few days. Since my brother was still
here, I decided I could make it if he went with me.

It was a first step for me on my own so to speak without Bill.
We traveled to Lahina by ferry and attended the celebrations. I rode
in the parade with Bill's drum and a friend, but without him. I don't
know how I did it because I was still in shock and 'not there'; and
constantly fought back tears remembering the parade we were on the
float together.

2008 Maui Canoe Festival Parade

I played his drum at the launching of the canoes. I stared at Bill's empty chair they had placed in the circle of carvers to honor him during the Awa Ceremony I was in a trance –not all here in this reality.

I sat with Molokai people at the dinner where the awards to the carvers were given out after dinner. I was 'blanked out' so to speak for I didn't hear my name called to come up and accept the Bill Kapuni paddle they were giving to the carvers for the 11th annual Maui Canoe Festival. I even remember seeing some of the carvers motioning me to come up on stage, but I just moved back further away blending into the crowd surrounding the stage. I was not 'present'. It reminded me of a time in law school when I almost broke from pressure a professor was placing on me in class. I could see everything, but I couldn't hear anything.

There were beautiful memories of us together everywhere I looked. Our love and laughter walked with me, but was surreal. The present wasn't real for me. The past was. I walked around and was comforted by many people who knew and loved Bill. I could see that they were also grieving at the loss of an important part of Hawaii.

Bill's friend had completed Bill's final drum. He told me they placed a program of his celebration inside the last drum as a remembrance. Although it is beautiful, it was different than if Bill had finished it. I knew Bill's work. I remembered when Bill started that drum, and here it was finished and he didn't finish it. "The drums really made themselves," Bill would say. They told him how deep they wanted to be and what carvings they wanted on them.

After my brother left Molokai, I slipped into a numbness where I was barely here. He had been very supportive for me and held me up with his kindness and caring while staying with me. I barely remember that time. I was so deep in my sense of loss and wanted to go with Bill. The days drifted by. I lost 15 pounds. I sat in a chair and stared out the window. I hardly ate anything but candy and cake and drank at least six cokes a day to keep my mood elevated with the caffeine and sugar. I spent a lot of time sitting in a chair, crying and trying to pray.

The first two weeks out, I was lower emotionally then I have ever been in my life, and I prayed to God to let me go with Bill. I had never before wished to die let alone prayed to die. I didn't want to be here in this world without him and was having difficulty coming back to this time and space without him.

In early June one night at 7:30 pm, somehow I turned on the IZ song "'n dis life" and began to dance with Bill like we used to. Because I was not all in this material world, and I had reached for the spiritual world to survive this, I could feel him through the veil between our different dimensions. There is a thin veil like the thickness of a silk slip between dimensions. Although I could not see him, (I rarely have the gift of sight), I could feel him next to me and as we danced, I physically became warm where he was holding me.

After that night, the mo'os chirped at 7:30pm every night and our dancing continued at about the same time each night for over a year, and as I would feel him next to me I would cry. I still cry, just not as long or hard when we dance now.

I could feel Bill and actually became frightened one of the first times I could feel him through that thin veil. He was so happy that I could recognize him and feel his presence, he started bumping into me a little and turning me around like we used to gently rough house when he was alive in the physical world. I said, "Who are you? Stop." When I thought about being frightened, he immediately stopped. I thought I knew it was Bill when he stopped so suddenly, but I didn't think Bill would be able to push me around like that from where he was. His energy is powerful and he seems to be able to move with the swiftness of a martial artist in play.

I think because he was so much in the spiritual world when he was in this world and we shared that strong spiritual connection, we are able to bridge across the two places we now occupy. I remember after he first passed when friends would visit me at dinner time at about 7:30 the mo'os (Geckos) around the house would start making noise, and I would politely ask my friends to leave. Bill was king of the mo'os (Kua Mo'o) and it was time for Bill and I to dance.

Although it was very difficult to see people without tearing up, it was good for me to get out to the Homesteader meetings. Many kind Hawaiians were trying to help me make it through this time. I received invitations to graduation parties and weddings, but couldn't leave the house.

After that, It was my comfort zone to at least be surrounded by his personal things and artwork in our home. I left his four pairs of shoes (sandals, two pairs of rubber clogs and sneakers) still outside the door as he had left them, until they disintegrated in the sun. It became paramount for me to be near his beautiful artwork. I could feel his mana from it now. When he was alive, his personal presence and spirit overwhelmed the mana in his art, and I paid very little attention to it. Now it was the most important thing in my life to have around me.

The third week out, I was 'pushed' into going to Saturday market which Bill and I had often frequented to buy our fruits and vegetables, and Bill would always go to Ameron's booth and try and trade with him for one particular shell lei necklace. He was looking at one particular three colored (burgundy, kahelelani and cross hatched) three strand necklace; and the last time we went to the market together, he put it on me and asked me if I liked it. I said, "Of course, but it's too expensive". He took it off of my neck and returned it to Ameron.

The shells used to make these pieces are extremely small. They are called Ni'i hou shells after the little Island off the coast of Kauai, where they are found; but Molokai has them also and Ameron free dives for them off Molokai and picks them up in the nooks and crannies of the reef. After he free dives for them, they have to be washed and sorted by color. The color of the shell is determined by where the animal lives. Because of their tiny size, they are hard to work with and it takes a great number to make one strand. For these reasons, they are expensive.

I saw Ameron as I crossed the street this Saturday morning and began to walk towards him. He was putting his tent away in its casing and looked up as I approached. He said something told him to look up as I was approaching. He respectfully expressed his condolences at my husband's passing which I was not able to handle very well yet; I would either tear up or look down and say nothing when someone would say something about Bill, or I would mumble a Thank You out from my bowed head.

He asked me to come back to their RV parked behind the buildings where his wife and children were waiting. He explained that Bill had come to him several times that spring to trade for this particular necklace, and he described it as he pulled it out of his inventory box. He stated that although his business was doing well, and he had sold lots and lots of necklaces; since the time my husband picked up that three strand necklace to trade for a present for me, it had not sold. Many many other necklaces he had made after that one had sold.

He said Bill not only came to the booth three or four times trying to negotiate with him for the necklace, but Bill stopped him whenever he saw him and asked him to come to the house for a trade. Bill did not have that kind of money. He traded for things he wanted – that was the old Hawaiian way. Ameron said not only did this necklace not sell; but after Bill picked it up to look at it the first time, no one ever even picked it up to look at it again!

He continued and said that he and his wife had talked about it and decided that it was only meant for me. That was why it had not sold. They further decided to gift it to me! I cried. I felt joy and thankfulness at their generosity; and having this the last present Bill gave me through them was simply overwhelming for me.

I eventually began to visit the Vertex to pray and be thankful for the Island. My thankfulness eventually grew to being thankful for the world, nature, heavenly bodies and finally my life itself. Being grateful for my life was the last. With that prayer, I had to think why I was still here and not gone also.

The Pyramid

CHAPTER FIFTY-ONE

BILL AND I LIVED IN SPIRIT most of the time, and during the last months, we were closer and higher living in spirit and not in the time and space of this physical world. I was having trouble coming back to the here and now. I wanted to be with him, and I knew were he was. I wanted to be there too. I remember during those early weeks wondering how I will feel next month, in three months, in six months? The change was not rapid. I did not notice any difference at all after three months. Part of each of us remained with the other. The separation of the physical occurred May 17th, but the spiritual separation we could not complete because we were and are one in Spirit.

Prior to his death, Bill visited friends on Sundays after church or on Saturdays. Looking back, I realize now, he was saying goodbye to people. One of those friends we visited on Island before Bill's death, I had run into at the Canoe Festival in Lahina while waiting for the ferry to return to Molokai. He stewards a fishpond on the East side of Molokai while teaching tourists a little about Hawaiian culture, all the while preserving and perpetuating Hawaiian culture. He asked me to come and see him when I returned to Molokai. I told him I would.

One morning I went to the Vertex to pray and his face kept coming in on me in my vision. I didn't really want to drive to see him so I pushed him out of my vision. I came inside and played the piano, which always used to be an enjoyment for me as I competed and was offered a college music scholarship by a judge when I was young. The playing always helped me get some of my emotions out. Tears flowed and I could feel Bill sitting with me in the yellow chair like he had done so many times before. He enjoyed my playing. The last time I played for him was an improvisation that was extremely heavy and sad. I believe now that it was my farewell concert for him. We both looked at each other after and then quickly looked down to avoid tears. I know I knew he was leaving, but I just couldn't bear bringing it to the conscious level.

After a while, even playing the piano, this friend of Bill's started appearing to me again. I shut the piano lid covering the keys and said, "Ok I'll go". I packed up the dogs and took them with me. I had no idea where he lived, and he was often not at the fishpond. But that day, he was there.

He was glad to see me and invited me to sit at a picnic table in the shade. I sat across from him. I did not know him very well, only that he was a friend of Bill's. I am a direct person and know Hawaiians are not always. It may take them an hour or more to get to the matter for a visit. That is because in their culture, time is not rushed and it is important to talk story and connect with the person you are visiting. I explained why I had come this day with my visions of him at the vertex and playing the piano, and asked him straight out "there must be a reason I am here. This is Molokai. You must have something to say to me, what is it?"

He, being a spiritual Hawaiian, needed to get a sense of my spirit before he responded; for he, likewise, only knew me through Bill. He placed his hands on my hands to feel my mana; and when he was satisfied with his knowledge, he asked me what I would be doing with Bill's art work? I said I had decided to give it to a museum so all could enjoy it not just me. He asked me where? I said I didn't know. He said "What about Molokai?" I received confirmation from spirit that this should happen. Bill would like that – it was his Island, the Island he chose to live and die on, so I told him, "Yes, it should stay on Molokai."

Bill had not given me any specific direction about his art, and leaving it totally up to me what I wanted to do with it. He would say, "If you need the money, sell it." But through this one friend of Bill's, I was now guided to start a Bill Kapuni museum. All his art went into Trust and I began to work on the idea of his art being in a museum.

Before Bill died, Puna had come to Molokai to see us and brought with her some friends from Switzerland. They were trying unsuccessfully to have a child. Bill told them about the special phallic rock on the north side of Molokai. Legend has it that if a woman sleeps under this rock, she will become pregnant. Bill and the husband, exchanged gifts when they parted.

Three months later Bill died, and I sent them a newspaper clipping of his passing and described what I wanted to do to honor my husband and his work. The husband replied stating that his wife was pregnant; and that Bill, in their short time together, had taught him "how to be a man". He felt very indebted to Bill and sent a donation. Come fall, he sent a picture of their new born baby!

Bill and several homesteaders had made a trip to Washington several years before, and had attended the opening of the new building called the Native American Cultural Museum, which contained, on the third floor, an exhibit of Hawaiian art on loan from other museums; because the Smithsonian had acquired no Hawaiian art to date. Bill had told me about this exhibit and years later was still enthusiastic about Hawaiian art having an entire floor at the Smithsonian.

Unfortunately, a Bill Kapuni museum, at least on our homestead was not to be. At first the idea was enthusiastically accepted but later, some of the homesteaders blocked my magnanimous gesture, and I found myself pushed into another direction. One of my classmates was in the Whitehouse during the Bill Clinton years, and I called her for names of the appropriate people to contact at the Smithsonian Institution in Washington, D.C.

After receiving the material from me that they requested, they fast tracked me and put me on the agenda of the next meeting. It only took them that meeting to view his work and decide they wanted it. They chose 15 pieces just based on the presentation of slides and descriptions I had sent them.

Because at that time they had no funding, I gifted them the pieces because it is my intention to preserve the Hawaiian culture and enable people throughout the world to learn from and enjoy Bill's art. Bill Kapuni is the first Hawaiian artist ever chosen for inclusion in their collection at the Smithsonian. Throughout his entire life Bill enjoyed teaching, so through his mana expressed in his extraordinary art, he will be able to continue to teach and share his Hawaiian culture with all.

Bill standing with his tallest piece — La La'au Mo Olele O Kahuna Kalaiwa A (The Spiritual Staff of the Kahuna That Guides the Canoe Builders)

CHAPTER FIFTY-TWO

After Bill's death, the biggest emotional boost for me was to be with and travel to the other Hawaiian Islands as an appointed member to the Sovereign Council of Hawaiian Homesteads Assembly. These were the Hawaiians I had seen many times over the years when Bill, (President and founder of our Association), and I traveled to meetings and kept up with Hawaiian issues and particularly Homestead issues. This summer, instead of a general convention in Honolulu, the Council traveled to each Island as an outreach to the Hawaiian Homesteaders.

The facts stated in the following three paragraphs are gleaned from the book entitled "Who owns the Crown Lands of Hawaii?" By Jon M. Van Dyke.

In 1893, the United States illegally overthrew the Kingdom of Hawaii which had been governed in a highly organized monarchy beginning with King Kamehameha I, who united the Hawaiian Islands in 1810. Queen Liliokalani under protest was locked up in her palace and forced to yield, in writing, her authority over the Hawaiian Islands "until such time as the United States shall undo their action..." she added to the document she signed.

With no declaration of war and no shot being fired, the United States government who, for business and political reasons, wrongfully took the Hawaiian Islands away from the monarchy and the Hawaiians, 'gave back' some of the Hawaiian land in 1920 in Trust for Hawaiian beneficiaries defined as "not less than one-half part of the blood of the races inhabiting the Hawaiian Islands previous to 1778 when the first foreigners landed on Hawaiian shores".

In 1986 the 50% Hawaiian koko descendants who had been awarded homestead land from this trust formed homesteader association groups on each Island; and they joined in turn forming a state council to speak for all of them with one voice for their Hawaiian interests.

In 2005 I was the first non-Hawaiian appointed to this Council of Hawaiian Homesteads. I brought to their circle a different perspective and a little legal perspective to their affairs. Since I understood and lived the culture with Bill and was a retired attorney, they valued my advise and counsel. I had no vote, of course.

After marrying Bill so soon after I moved to Molokai, I immersed myself in Hawaiian culture, not only to make him happy, but to understand his culture so I could better understand him and Hawaiian issues. We mostly saw and were friends with Hawaiians. Many were my friends who now were standing behind me even without Bill. They did not view me with a white skin color. They saw me as a Hawaiian at heart they would call it, and they would say to me, "I am your friend".

CHAPTER FIFTY-THREE

HOW DID I, A PHILADELPHIA DEBUTANTE, an attorney, thrice married, arrive on Molokai and marry Bill Kapuni, a pure Hawaiian Kahuna, the love of my life, only to lose him? Because it was meant to be. I would not have changed a thing. We experienced a once in a lifetime love so I know it exists, just like I know Bill possessed remarkable powers of concentration, healing, and abstraction of thought – all gifts obtained by keeping near Nature; because Nature keeps the human spirit sensitive to impressions not commonly felt by most and keeps one in touch and in connection with unseen powers. I was able to connect with Bill, because I likewise had been most of my life sensitive to unseen powers that of the light of God and Nature all internally learned and ignited by my Grandmother and Father.

When you consider the earth, aina, and yourself as sacred all containing life within, it is easier to be patient and loving and kind to others and stay in the Light. You can assist others in bringing them out of the dark and onto a path of light by teaching them to honor the land and all living things created, thus, bringing them into harmony with God.

When one lives in the spiritual world in harmony with nature, you look for signs in nature all the time to guide you. Bill was taught about signs of nature by his Tutu, and he in turn taught me. I listen to the many lizards that live in and around the house, because Bill was "King of the Lizards", (Ku a Mo'o). They are like the dogs only the lizards send off the alarm before the dogs when someone is coming to the house; and dogs don't send off the alarm when someone significant to my life is about to call on the phone, the mo'os do. In Hawaiian culture, the Mo'o is their most spiritual being.

Bill's amakua were the Mo'o (Lizzard) and Lono (Shark). Mine are the Butterfly, Black Raven and Wolf. They are my spiritual amakua, and I am always attentive and aware of them for they cross your path only to tell you something significant for your life.

Hoku and Loki and Me

CHAPTER FIFTY-FOUR

FOR THE FIRST YEAR AND A half out, I endured many stresses from prejudice, jealousy, and sometimes hatred for no other reason then those persons thrust their own issues upon me for they were unable to resolve them within themselves—much like blaming another for your own problems of emotions.

On Molokai, Hawaii, the Hawaiian cultured thought is that dark spirits are immediately drawn to loud noises at night, and those spirits can influence you in negative ways and 'interfere' with your normal mental thinking process. I call it interference. In early summer, one Saturday night, some of my neighbors made great loud noises (fireworks and flying airplanes and weed eaters) from the house on the hill; and I was wondering why any Hawaiian would make such loud noises at night after sunset?

Bill told me to close all the windows and doors and I got out of bed to do so. The noise was so loud, I placed a pillow over my head to muffle the noise and wrapped my body in pillows and a quilt, and prayed. Then after I went to sleep, I was awakened by two terrible yelling fights up the road at two different houses. It was obvious to me that those people had not protected themselves against the dark spirits like I did.

I was up several times that night protecting myself, praying and reading the Bible. In the morning I was not able to walk the dogs further then the tree at the end of the road on the way to the Vertex. I was wiped out that whole day, exhausted from what I consider now to be a dark, negative spiritual activity that night outside in the neighborhood.

I feel certain that the noise was meant for me; and they believed I would be mentally injured, and perhaps physically, from what the noise brought forth. They obviously thought I was just another haole (foreigner) from the mainland and had no idea of my spiritual background experiences and beliefs, what I had learned from Bill, or why Bill and I were together.

That stopped when they figured out it wasn't hurting me, but only hurting their other neighbors. Then they began the drive bys I call them. I live on a cul-de-sac with no other houses on the street. People began driving up the cul-de-sac before and after work and at lunch time and in the morning. I had air let out of my tires. I had my car registration sticker taken off the car (twice) and the registration card taken out of the glove box!

By the end of July, I was noticing items disappearing from Bill's workshop…his tools, boxes, etc. and called the police on two occasions. I was told that 99% of robberies were neighbors or relatives. I eventually discovered they were right, and in August decided that I would need surveillance cameras installed to stop the stealing.

During this summer period, I was told some 'dark' kahuna people were also attempting to send negative energy my way in large doses. I felt and saw it sometimes. The harassment in conjunction with what I call 'interference' was so severe that it prevented me from going to church until I got the cameras up and could feel the property was safe when I left it.

Sometimes my water would be turned off to my automatic drip system, and it would take a while before I noticed it causing the plants, which Bill had started from cuttings, to suffer and many died. In addition, I noticed a change in my hot water heater temperature…. very hot one morning when I was almost scalded. A friend came over to check the timer and heater. The timer was missing one part now so that the heater was running all the time and driving my electricity bill up by 30% every month.

I bought what he said was missing, and he affixed it to the dial and, in addition, turned down the temperature which had been turned up from its original position at installation. I placed a lock on the box then so it couldn't be tampered with again and my bills returned to normal.

The gas valves under the house had been turned off so I couldn't cook until the gas co. came with a new canister that I didn't need. All that was needed was that the valve had to be turned back on. I never knew about things like that…outside was Bill's domain.

I had had trouble with hang up telephone calls and wrong numbers, and with my phone being tapped also, I bought a cell phone to alleviate those problems. I locked the box to the phone under the house after I had it checked for tapping. Someone would turn off my answering service to my land line from 5:00 pm Friday until 8:30 am Monday so I had no messages received over the weekend, which was my loneliest time, of course. Many people were calling to keep tabs on me, and I wasn't able to receive their calls of concern.

—m—

Bill's adopted daughter was pushing the Department of Hawaiian Homelands to get his lot and my house that I built for us on it and turned over to her! She didn't understand the house was mine and the land was in a Trust administered by the Department. She also didn't understand whoever the lease was awarded to would have to pay for the house which was mine. I could move the house if I wanted to and leave the land. To be a leaseholder, one has to have a certain Hawaiian blood quantum. She claimed she was his daughter neglecting to inform the Department that she was adopted and lacked any Hawaiian blood whatsoever. Fortunately, Bill's older brother who has integrity and a sense of what is right and still practices Hawaiian honor and protocol, put a stop to that nonsense.

I had been asked to come into the local Hawaiian Homes Department two weeks after my husband's death and was told I had to leave my home; because I lacked the necessary Hawaiian blood quantum! All this, and I was still in shock over my husband's death! I decided the people who were harassing and stealing from me were negative energies and cruel and the Department was insensitive to my grieving, and their policies were not pono with Hawaiian culture.

The land I built our home on was leased land from the Hawaiian Trust lands given Hawaii in 1920. My husband received a lease because he was well over 50% pure Hawaiian blood. (Bill was over 90% Hawaiian and of royal blood meaning his rights to the land were superior to the Department's administrative authority.) I told the Department I was not moving and gave them my legal reasons. They suggested a way I could stay without a five to six year court fight, which I had no desire for; because I did not want to hurt the Hawaiians in any way and a court fight may damage the Trust. I simply did not want to leave the house I built for my husband. Not only was it sacred land, it was the place I had envisioned spending the rest of my life with Bill on. We designed every inch of it. And I could still feel him there. I also told the Department, "I am grieving, why can't people just leave me alone and let me heal?"

Their suggestion, at the time was to have the appraisal done on the house and have a relative of Bill's take over the lease, and I could then stay under his lease. The person who suggested this was a friend of Bill's but subsequently retired before this could be accomplished.

With my desire to join my husband anyway, all of this going on and now with the added stress of fighting to continue living in our home, as I look back on it all, it is a wonder I am still here. How can I survive all this pilikia and the grieving?

The local harassment stopped for a short while but began again in the fall. Some of these 'harassers' were who I call Ranch people who blamed me for the Ranch closing and wanted to 'get even' from the La'au Point controversy. Actually as it turned out with the economy, the Ranch would have most likely closed anyway, and they would have lost their jobs a few months later. Fortunately, many were able to move off Island to better employment opportunities. They simply had negative 'interference' and would rather hate someone and blame that person for the loss of their job then take the time to think things through. They only had a sophomoric understanding of why Bill and I were together, they really had no clue.

CHAPTER FIFTY-SIX

DURING THE FIRST SIX MONTHS WITHOUT Bill, not only did I have to grieve for him in the deepest part of my core, because we were attached on so many levels; but I had to decide where to live, what to do with the house, his things etc. I had to first decide where I wanted to live. Even though I felt I belonged to the Island, several people were not making me feel welcome to say the least.

I made a trip to Kauai with the Sovereign Council of Hawaiian Homesteads Assembly in late summer and made the determination that Molokai was my place....even with all the negativity about my living on Hawaiian Homestead leased land. I belonged on Molokai just as Molokai had called me back to it and directed me to Bill. I now felt I belonged in the homestead space Bill and I had built… at least for now.

I no longer yearned for Kauai even though my friends there wanted me to return. My Molokai friends also wanted me to remain, but more importantly, my spiritual framework was now aligned with Molokai. Each Island has a different spirituality. This is his Island. I couldn't get him to move off it. Molokai was where I felt home since 1982 when I first stepped on the aina, and put in my will for my ashes to be strewn over the Island way back then in 1982.

This was a difficult decision, because I would have to fight to remain on the homestead not having Hawaiian koko (blood). The United States dictated how much Hawaiian blood you needed to be able to live on Hawaiian Trust lands. The 1920 Commission Act set forth laws some of which need to be revamped to take into account older surviving spouses like myself, who took their savings and built their Hawaiian spouse a home on Trust Lands so that he could finally live his dream. I made that happen for Bill. Fortunately, most Hawaiians respect elders and are considerate of an individual who was married to and cared for a Hawaiian. Many widows had been allowed to stay on the leased land until they pass. That is in accord with Hawaiian culture.

Bill had had his homestead lease since 1983. The land was sacred. He and a Hopi Indian had built an important medicine wheel on it. But it wasn't until I took a great deal of my money from savings and sale of my Molokai condo, and put it into our beautiful home, that he could live on his land. But no one could have foreseen that we would only have eight months to live in our home together.

CHAPTER FIFTY-SEVEN

I KEPT PULLING MYSELF UP OUT of the hole I was in with the help of God, Bill, prayer, going to church and my friends. I kept coming up and up little by little and then Christmas came when I was dashed down to the ground again. Christmas is hard for anyone who has lost someone, but when you lose the other half of yourself, it can be devastating. I had never been so alone. I had no joy and no love in my life and was going blind.

It came upon me suddenly after Christmas. I had developed cataracts in both eyes and all of the sudden couldn't see street signs or many other things I had taken for granted. There is a famous author and Spiritual Teacher named Louise Hay who wrote a book, titled "You Can Heal Your Life". It's about disease, its causes and remedies. She states the cause of cataracts and blindness is you have no joy in your life and see no future for yourself. This was exactly what I felt.....no joy and I didn't know what my future would be now that Bill was gone. I could "see" no future for myself here.

The first cataract operation was unsuccessful. Yet, I was blessed for not becoming blind in that eye. Somewhere from just before the surgery when the doctor checked my eyes and the day after surgery, my retina was torn in two places. The lazer was placed on an incorrect setting. I immediately went to a retina specialist who said almost everyone else that happens to goes blind instantly! One tear is sufficient stress placed on the retina to pull it away from the back of the eye wall, but two tears at 11 and 4 o'clock was grave. I had two tares. I was "sown up" by a laser, and I recovered sufficiently three months later to have the second eye done. The second eye surgery went well.

In the spring, I had recently completed a quantum spiritual growth when I simply meditated for three days straight without doing much of anything else but praying. When I was given a sedative in a vein in my hand before the second cataract operation Bill's energy appeared right in front of me about a foot from my face to get my attention. Then he moved up and back a few feet and reached out his hand for mine and said, "Come, come up with me." Because I totally trusted him and was never afraid of him, I took his hand and stepped up with him into a beautiful golden light with pastel colors of pink and blue and white all around. No detail, just like a pale water color painting of colors. I have no idea how long I was with him. I remember I felt very happy, peaceful, content, and knowing everything in my life was going to be all right. When I was awakened, the person behind me in the line of patients to be operated on had jumped ahead of me and was finished with her operation while I was away with Bill.

My Brother

CHAPTER FIFTY-EIGHT

My BROTHER CAME IN FEBRUARY TO visit because he felt I was in great need. This was his fourth visit to Molokai. The first was the wedding, the second was Christmas and the third was Bill's Celebration. I was in great need of support, for looking back then at myself, I had chosen my path to join my husband. I saw Bill in a vision waiting for me to join him at the place he wants us to be buried together. He was dressed in relaxed white pants and a beautiful shirt of a soft grayish shade of green with billowy sleeves and open neck like the white shirt he wore at our wedding. I had significantly gone downhill health wise and friends were calling me more frequently because they realized how I was going down. I had decided life was not bearable without him.

My brother realized I needed a change of scenery and took me on the ferry to Maui for two days and a night. I hadn't realized how much I needed a break from Molokai. I walked around Lahaina and enjoyed the sights. The memories of Bill were not so vivid and prominent this the third time over since his death. I walked to a theater to see a movie while my brother rested.

As dear as my Hawaiian friends are, they all are part of their families. This Island has a very unique population in that almost all Hawaiians here are related to a handful of families that go way back. They are all related to each other in some way.

There are a few newcomers to Molokai, but they usually have relatives that have lived here a very long time. Combine this with the emphasis in the Hawaiian culture about families, a newcomer like me who is not Hawaiian and no longer has a Hawaiian husband, is usually outside the Hawaiian social sphere. There are some notable exceptions for me of people who include me in their family activities.

Finally, some homesteader ladies about my age started looking out for me in the spring and that started the changing of public opinion of me on Island. They are both kupunas and prominent women of prominent families. In Hawaiian culture, kupunas, (older citizens) are respected for their opinions and guidance in the society. Hawaiians believe in the wisdom of their elders. They follow them. The Hawaiians who were seemingly against me were considerably younger and less mature, and neither grounded in wisdom nor very spiritual. They may also have been looking at the situation in a very dualistic way. I am a white woman on Hawaiian land. The Kupunas are able to recognize a Hawaiian heart and accept the connection of people with aloha. They also remember how actively I helped protect their land.

These ladies decided to step in when a part Hawaiian friend of Bill's ex-girlfriend yelled at me in the Hawaiian complex "why are you still here? You're not Hawaiian! You don't belong here. Why don't you leave?" These ladies did not like that and decided they would have to try and do something about it, because they 'wanted me to stay' on Island and told me so.

This was not Hawaiian aloha culture and as nasty and bigoted as it was, it drew attention to the problem I was facing on Island with the two factions—former Ranch employees and friends of his X girl friend. This is a small Island and between those two groups who had already been talking "stink' about me, it was an up hill climb for me to stay in Light.

Such anger and prejudice, and they didn't even know me! That's what I couldn't understand. How could they have such hate when they didn't even know me? I was experiencing reverse discrimination. The blacks before 1964 must have felt the same way. The Jewish girls from my school, who, even though their parents could afford it, were not invited to most of the debutante parties. I had never understood it then and I don't understand the prejudice against me now.

There were also people who were being retaliatory. I had accepted the challenge of controversy when I wrote the La'au questions. Bill said they would come after me for it. But I replied, "I have to do it". He was right and the timing was such that he wasn't here to protect and defend me now. If he were alive, the harassment would not have occurred at all. It was my passion to save this Island....the last truly Hawaiian Island, that drove me to write the questions, and I told Bill I had to do it. I had to try and save the Island. Black Raven taught me about my dreams of prophecy and which ones were set in the future and which ones could still be changed. My dream of the beach had been a future not set in stone. It had been a dream that could still be changed and I had been called upon to help change it.

The second wave of harassment started in the fall and ended in February. The drive bys were less. The police had talked to the two women who would park across from my house and walk around the neighborhood even though they lived up the hill. I had begun to take license plate numbers on the drive bys and their license plate belonged to a truck not the car they were driving. The police discovered them anyway and that stopped. I knew things were bad when my church prayed for me and my homestead one Sunday, and the police started coming by the house periodically.

The harassment reduced when Bill's hanai cousin from the East end said "We should get guns on the lanais and have a standoff". (I smiled a little at the thought of someone looking out for me.) These few people had ignited the Island so much against me! I still held my ground spiritually and my church was supporting me with prayers. Bill and the spirits around the pyramid on the ag lot, strongly supported me.

The third wave of harassment was in April and was short. It was drive-bys. The Island had already turned my way, and I received smiles from most people now instead of the usual cold shoulder and scowls. I was, for the first time, enjoying how nice Molokai can be. It made me happy, and I looked forward to going to town instead of dreading it during the shunning periods that had accompanied those waves.

In March for Prince Kuhio Day the homesteaders always get together for a celebration of the Prince who gave up his Hawaiian heritage to become a legislator and lead the US Congress to set aside

Hawaiian lands for Hawaiians to homestead. The year before Bill had barbequed teriyaki beef to make money for our Homestead Association. It was a great effort for him for he was only going to live seven more weeks. Looking back, I see that he was saying goodbye to them all in his way.

This year, since I was a homesteader and officer in the Association, I decided to go and see if it made me feel better. A few cultured kupuna Hawaiians had told me the week before that Bill was coming to them and talking to them. I knew that because he was not always around the house now. He was out doing things. I can only assume he was asking them to help me.

Two well respected ladies who were the dignitaries of the event, asked me to sit with them at their table. It was an honor for me to be included in their circle. One had lost her husband the year before and she was struggling also so we had a great deal in common to talk about. She later asked me if things had gotten better for me and I replied yes. The reason was because they were publicly showing everyone they accepted me and others should follow their direction as Kupuna.

CHAPTER FIFTY-NINE

Bill was Hawaiian and didn't care much about money. He didn't have checking accounts and only one savings account with $35 when he died...no insurance, social security, pension -- nothing. For ancient and traditional Hawaiians money was not important. Theirs was a life that always lived in connection with Nature and Nature's bounty. Everyone had what they needed. Bill Kapuni lived this Hawaiian culture of his ancestors.

Even if I knew all the stress of harassment and uncertainty I would be under during this first year out, I would still marry him all over again. He taught me that most in life is more important than money. Before moving to Hawaii, money had always been very important to me, because I didn't want to be a 'bag lady in my old age.' I was very careful to avoid that fear of poverty. All my banking and finance courses in college came to the forefront of my brain as I plowed through my life's trails accumulating, in small increments, my hard earned money. I started working at sixteen in a florist shop and never really stopped until I came to Molokai and met Bill Kapuni.

I had to learn that money can imprison you and keep you from living in the now. If you focus on money you lose the possibility of living in the now with God. I had placed an important value on it when my father died, and I was left penniless; or when I had $250 to my name after my first divorce. Bill taught me the 'power of gold' is a false god. Money for him was a non entity. He lived in and loved Nature and his art throughout his life. Money had no emotional value to him and so it came for me the same.

This Hawaiian part of my life was the learning experience about love and money and the final portion of control lessons also. Money is merely an energy to be used for the purpose of joy and living our lives in harmony, love and Light. In Hawaii, as Bill Kapuni's wife, I learned the value of money can not begin to compare with living in love and spirit. I am grateful for the learning experience and change it made in me. True love it is! You simply stop right there because there is nothing else to compare or desire. It is what you've been searching for and now you know your search is over. You have all you need.....finally at long last.

It was all meant to be. Bill set me free from the power of gold as our song says. He certainly did.

Love is all there is.

I had been frugal all my life and denied myself simple pleasures like stopping at an ice cream parlor on the way home because it would cost a few dollars. I spent money freely on him and us for our living in the now and enjoying life. I am grateful I did that because we lived life to its fullest not wasting a minute of our joy together.

CHAPTER SIXTY

I HAD LEARNED LOVE IN MY marriage to Bill Kapuni. We both did. Neither of us had ever loved anyone in our lives more then we loved each other. True love makes all fear, guilt, anger, hate, distrust melt away. It falls off you like dropping your robe to the floor. We, finally, at our late ages found who we were meant to love forever. We lived in love through the spirit of God.

We had both learned the issue of control in our marriage also. Neither of us tried to control the other or circumstances surrounding us. We gave up the illusion of believing we have any control over anyone or any situation except ourselves and simply lived in Spirit in God's Love.

Living in God's love in spirit is like living in the flow of a river running above us, and all we have to do is move up and catch it. I used to describe moving into spirit (life force) was like grabbing the handles on a trolley or bus that keeps you from falling. Indeed. Spirit keeps you from falling, but more importantly you grab the handle and pull yourself up to catch the flow of spirit and you travel along on your journey in the river. I think it could also be described as catching the wind in your sail. The wind carries you along. When you are in this flow of life, you are not separate, you are part of the flow—part of Spirit – part of God....and not alone.

When you are in love and in Spirit you are part of everything. You have no separateness. You have no priorities, you just are. You are living in the moment without time or space. The deepest Bill and I ever were in love and spirit was when he was dying. There was no time or space. We simply were together in Spirit. We were one in

Spirit -- there was no separation from each other. There was nothing between us. Only Oneness. Oneness with God.

Oneness is a sacred word. I never realized that before. Oneness is all there is. It is like those mystical experiences I had with nature all those years ago; and now I was alone with another human being not in nature this time, but with my Husband. Bill and I always knew there was no time when you are in the moment in Spirit or with God. You simply are one with all there is.

Time and space are really only terms assigned to this physical world. When you are living with a watch, you are squarely in the middle of this physical world. When you realize you don't need a watch to live, you are moving toward living in God's love with no time. Living in the moment without time does not require space either. It is simply a place of oneness with yourself and God.

I guess that is why I had such a time overcoming Bill's death and moving forward with my life alone. In our relationship, we were no longer searching for anything because we didn't want anything else anymore. When you find true love, you just stop. During so much of our lives together, there was nothing else but each other. We didn't see anyone but each other. We hardly saw anything at all but each other. Our energies connected and became one in Spirit. Our sex was even in Spirit. That is why it was so exceptional and like nothing either one of us had ever experienced before. We prayed before our sex to ensure we would be in Spirit.

During the last few months we would drive to east or west end of the Island for a ride and rarely noticed the spectacular scenery. It was all part of us.... part of our oneness and our connection to all there is. When you are able to be one with each other, Nature, God, Universe, Cosmos, all you have is pure Joy. These were our last days together. We had great Joy at the point of separating into different worlds because we were one and not separate and knew the 'we' of us would continue on for eternity. We are connected to all there is – the Universe – the Cosmos – all.

Fear of death was something I had conquered with the near drowning two times, walking fire, repelling, running rapids, and living through an abusive relationship. Bill learned his through fights growing up, abused as a child, and almost drowning three times: once in a big wave while surfing, and the first at the hands of a younger brother; and the last time diving off the shores of Molokai. Needless to say he addressed his fear of dying with the courage of a Hawaiian warrior. With dignity, strength and valor he proceeded through the days until I was finally able to let him go. He hung on for me until I was able to accept our parting for a while.

CHAPTER SIXTY-ONE

BILL AND I WERE SO OPPOSITE in many ways (masculine, feminine, Hawaiian, Caucasian, dark skin, light skin, brown eyes, blue eyes, under educated, over educated, socialite, living on the beach, use of light and dark energy sources); yet we were one in our love for each other and when we were in Spirit with God, we were in Joy, Love and Light. When in Spirit we were one without time and space. We were one with God—opposites, but one with God. How could that be in a dualistic framework (of good and bad, light and dark etc.) that we have all learned in our society?

The only way that it can be, I decided, is that we are all One and living in One Life Force, Spirit together and all made by the same God. Since He made first the dark without form or void, and then he made the light, surely he made light and dark people. We all live within the same God. We are all in Spirit together as One.

The reason we are all in one Spirit is because the Creator made dark first and then the light...that includes all we can know. And everything he made was very good. (Genesis 1. 31) He made it ALL and it was very good. Both dark and light, good and bad are all very good. Hence there is no duality. It is all one and all good. God never separated light and dark, good and bad. He never said the dark was bad and the light good. He said everything he made was very good.

Everything in the physical form (including our bodies) are bits and pieces of the interstellar material from the sun's formation, and all heavy elements (excluding hydrogen and helium) are forged and recycled in the cores of stars. (Recovering the Sky in the Western Intellectual Tradition, Joseph,

R. D., presented at the 9th East-West Philosophers Conference, University of Hawaii, 2005). In other words, matter is all inclusive within itself. Since our material bodies are all unified, why then wouldn't our spirits likewise be unified as one, as well?

Because he made man in his image and likeness, if man is both good and bad, God, likewise must be good and bad, because God made man in his image and likeness. This is all true if we believe in the duality of good and bad. However, if we know intuitively God is good, then we can accept everything that was created is good. All that God created is included in the one all knowing loving encompassing God. We are all part of that one Supreme good God. When we use our dualistic thinking patterns, we mistakenly see or make a judgment about someone or something as bad. It is really all good made by the Creator, and all One.

Bill's first year anniversary (of passing) May 17th was fast approaching. As I approached May 1st, the dread of last year's events set in. I started vividly remembering the days of last year and going through the pain again of watching my husband suffer and continue on his path of leaving me. As each day came I remembered: the Thursday he stopped eating, Mother's day when he went to Honolulu for the last time, and the last week of his life at home in hospice.

Bill died on Hula Pico day. The day of celebrating the Hula, which was born on Molokai. I went to the public talk about it on Thursday evening where I was extended an invitation to attend a private sacred hula ceremony held on sacred mountain ground the next day. I was very honored and knew I would be in a spiritual place soon -- a ceremony with just Kumu's family and his Halaus.

It was a very special day. I had mentally and spiritually prepared myself for this special ceremony and was high in spirit when I left the house forgetting my kihei Bill had made. I was glad someone was able to give me a black one appropriate for mourning Bill. Protocol is extremely important to Hawaiian ceremony.

After being pointed to the front row for a place to sit Thrusday evening, I had unknowingly sat next to Kumu's mother. During your journey, there are some people with whom you immediately connect as you speak your first words to each other. She was one. After the Halau ceremony Friday, she came up to me right after as though we had been friends a long time. She had lost her husband five years earlier and recognized my grief. She was very spiritual and perceptive, and we talked a very long time. The spiritual high from this hula ceremony and the sacredness of this land took me right into the next morning.

I knew the 17th would be a most difficult day and I just kept thinking, if I can only make it to that day, I will have reached a mile stone. Some friends told me about the first year anniversary of a death of a loved one where in Hawaiian culture, everyone gathers to assess each other's progress and wish him well as he ascends to be with his ancestors for further teaching. I certainly didn't want him to leave me more then he had already been doing since April when I completed a large spiritual growth, and he began to leave me for longer periods of time during the day (returning at night). Since I didn't have much family, for a paina (family gathering around food), I called my best friends and asked some of Bill's best friends also. Most often they coincided in the same person. Some people came at 11am to help me get ready. I needed help. Some people brought leis and flowers. Others brought food. They left at 7 pm.

Bill's hanai mom and someone in her family put together a short movie of Bill from when they first met him when he was 19. I shared this movie with all who came that day. This short movie captures not only the 'olden days of Hawaii' which everyone longs for, but it captured the incredible spirit of aloha that belonged only to Bill in his special way. The movie puts a smile on your face as you see him completely joyful and free. It is how I picture him with a smile that covered his entire face. I would have been too shy to talk to him when he was a young surfer, for he was far too handsome.

Then people, who hadn't been to our home, asked me to talk about Bill's art work which overwhelms you from every nook and cranny. There is really too much of his art and some pieces are too big to be properly displayed in a house. People are always amazed at the extensive variety of his work. His talent to make any traditional Hawaiian art was exceptional.

We then ate the lovely dishes everyone brought and settled in for talking story. Some people shared memories with Bill. Others were silent. Then we moved outside on the lanai where two people bringing ukuleles played lovely Hawaiian melodies. We sang, and the music wafted out to the neighborhood.

Everyone felt Bill with us and all were happy in each other's company once again celebrating the life of this remarkable man I just happened to marry. There were several blessings of the day. It was cloudy to keep the un-airconditioned house cool, it rained tears from heaven to help us with our grief, the clouds opened up to let three shafts of light shine before us touching the aina, and then we were left with a rainbow.

As I sat by myself after the guests left I thought about my Dad. He hadn't meant to leave me any more than Bill had. I learned so much from him that helped me live the extraordinary life I have lived.

My Dad lived by the philosophy of Dr. Norman Vincent Peale, and his book "The Power of Positive Thinking"; and my Dad taught me to do the same. Think positive, because thinking can make it so. Your thoughts can create the energy and reality around you. You can create your own reality by thinking it. Deny yourself entertaining any negative thoughts.

You can heal that way -- deny the negative illusion of illness and see only the positive light energies. Don't ask to 'fix' or 'cure' anyone, simply ask for it to be as God created it and intended it to be...perfect. Simply affirm that the event, person, or circumstance as being in Spirit, Light, as it was intended to be from the beginning, from the Creator.

Have good intention with all you do in your life. Use positive energies, positive words said to each other, and positive descriptions of people and things. Take action on the positive energy momentum of the present. It is said Healers see the past and future as the same in the now, for the future when experienced is already in the now soon to be in the past. I heal in the now in God's Light.

Both of us conquered fear which takes great courage and complete willingness to walk directly into the fear in order to dissipate and dissolve it. When you are able to accomplish this, your growth will be great and your path will be a little easier. Because both of us were athletic, we were used to walking into physical situations without fear and that helped us overcome fears in life. For both of us, after we learned spiritual and unconditional love with and for each other, we realized that life without love is no life at all. The greatest of everything we can know is Love. God is Love. Love is all there is!

PRAYER

Oh God,
You are above and beneath me in the heavens
You are with me in the four directions of the wind
You encircle me all around in the air I breath
with your Love
You surround me with the earth, waters and
every living thing
You are ALL there is.
Light within me a love for all things,
Light within me to see love in all things.
Teach me to know we are all one with you
Teach me to know we are all within the One
The Oneness of you, O God

CPSIA information can be obtained
at www.ICGtesting.com
Printed in the USA
FSHW02n1206180518
48341FS